Cutting Through To Success

Third Edition

Learning For The Leader Inside Of You!

Deborah R. Monroe

Cutting Through To Success: Learning For The Leader Inside Of You!
by Deborah R. Monroe

Copyright © 2024 by Deborah R. Monroe. All rights reserved. Printed in the USA on sustainably harvested paper. No part of this book may be copied or reproduced in any form without express written consent of the publisher and author except in the case of brief quotations embodied in critical articles and reviews.

For information, contact
BDI Publishers, Atlanta, Georgia
bdipublishers@gmail.com

Layout Design: Tudor Maier

BDI Publishers

Atlanta, Georgia

ISBN: 978-0-9889330-1-9

Dedication to My Guide:

For the Wisdom, the Kindness,

the Optimism and the Gratefulness…

No Regrets!

To The Cinna-Man

whose edification and appreciation

lifts My heart and life.

Acknowledgements

For all those along the way who have influenced me, taught me, held me in their arms, made me laugh, caught me when I cried, whether still an active part of my life or not, you have all taught me something, everything has been valuable, even if it was painful in the "going-through".

With a grateful and humble heart, I want to acknowledge my support system of smart and loyal friends here on earth and those who have gone ahead into Grace:

Alisa Garber, Annie Coetzee, Blair Steinbach, Randy Celaya, Carina Fiedeldey-Van Dijk, Cheryl Rayfield, Kenny Forget, Keplyn Robinson, Lea Brovedani, Marla Persky, Pieter Van Jaarsveld, Sharon Lewis, Tatiana Ryjova

My family, who through our good times and growing times, never fail to impart wine, wisdom, truth and who, more than they know, hold my tender heart in their hands: *Mom, Dad, Sandy, David and Kathy and of course my heart and love, Evan.*

To those pioneers of wise men and women from whom I harvest truth, your work has influenced me and will continue to impact others. I thank you:

Adele Lynn, Annie Mckee, Brent Darnell, Bruce Peltier, Daniel Pink, Daniel Goleman, David Allen, David Rock, Elizabeth Miles, John Medina, Joseph Jaworski, Joshua Freeman, Joyce Meyer, Kaleel Jamison, Malcolm Gladwell, Marshal Rosenberg, Martin Seligman, Paul Ekman, Paul Herr, Peter Salovey, Richard Boyatzis, Timothy Ferriss, My 6 Seconds Emotional Intelligence Community, My IHHP Coaching Peers, My RED Family

A Special Thank You to My beautiful Partner, the surprise of My life.

A Special Thank You to Laurel Quinones, Julia Weis and Sandy Weis who came a'runin' when I had a great need.

Side Note: At one point or another, I had to make a decision to send this second edition to print knowing full well that this book may contain grammatical or spelling slip-ups, for which I ask you to make a note of and email our office. You can help us be better! Our editors made a valiant effort to correct the previous editor's errors. Nothing is perfect on this earth and thank you for your understanding!

Table Of Contents

Introduction..7

Blade #1: Honor Myself...19

Blade #2: Manage My Distractions..37

Blade #3: Get Myself a Coach..57

Blade #4: The Art of Listening...69

Blade #5: What is Coming Out of My Mouth?....................................85

Blade #6: Build My Relationships..103

Blade #7: Manage My Thought Life...125

Blade #8: Let Go and Delegate...149

Blade #9: Reduce Stress and Get Creative..165

Blade #10: Kindness is the Fertilizer That Makes Things Grow...........185

Blade #11: Review of the Year..195

Appendix A: Accountability Coach Guidelines...................................209

Appendix B: List of Emotions..211

Appendix C: List of Human Needs..213

Appendix D: Things to Consider List!..214

Introduction

If I had eight hours to chop down a tree, I'd spend six sharpening my axe.
— *Abraham Lincoln*

Dad's Knives

My dad always gave us the strangest wisdom when growing up. One cold evening, as a teenager, when we were living in England, he got out his long knife sharpening steel and began carefully sliding the blade of his favorite carving knife up and down the long metal rod. I could see his concentration; one stroke on this side, another on that side. He looked up at me and with great seriousness spoke these words, *"the most dangerous knives to use are dull knives…you always want to make sure they are sharp. More people get seriously hurt when they use a dull blade."*

Of course, my response to this as I got older was to always have sharp knives in the house. Within my relationship with my brother there seems to be this odd competition. It is a knife "feeling" competition….". Feel how *sharp* that blade is," he says to me every time he gets a new knife. There is always a gleam in his eye as his thumb swiftly waves back and forth friskily on the cutting edge of his new blade.

Little did I know that as I grew into the person I am today, that this life lesson from Dad would be an analogy for the work I do and the people I come into contact with on a daily basis.

In our work lives and elsewhere, we tend to approach our days with dull blades and dirty tools. The drive for productivity in North America, struggles against real or imagined competitors in Europe and Asia causing us to sleep less, eat food that doesn't keep us fit, and work too many hours as we submit to a culture of corporate slavery. Our creativity and inventiveness, clarity of mind, brain energy all suffer under the "operational details" we get caught in every day, therefore, limiting our time and energy on thinking and acting strategically for the future. Let's stop this madness or at least limit it for our sanity and the view of our future successes!

Take Care Of Your Tools

> *"Good tools will last your lifetime if you take care of them"*
> *— Everyone's Grandpa*

We all know how important it is to take care of our tools. We know this by the attention given to men/women with the most inventive and beautiful tool-storage systems in the world!

A contractor friend of mine would say to me, "Deborah, the job is easy if you have the right tools". The tools need not only to be present, they must be functional and we need to know how to use them. It is no fun to think you are going to cut tile for that long overdue project in the bathroom; go get the tile cutter, plug it in and find that the engine is frozen and the blade will not turn. The moment of frustration arises and more than likely some four-letter word will flow freely out of the mouth as you look for your local hardware store credit card and the keys for the mini-van…then off you go, wasting time, energy and money…just because the tool was not cleaned or cared for.

The self-help books on how to cut and set tile may not be as valuable as you think. Something else to consider is that most of us do not learn by reading…we are hands on, kinesthetic and tactile learners. Let me get my hands dirty, let me try it first…or show me some darn pictures in the instruction booklet.

Think of Starbucks! After every café latte or cappuccino, one of the things you notice is the milk-frother device being wiped down completely. They even have a specific rag they use for the job. If they didn't take the time to clean that piece of equipment off it would not last long!

We take the time to have the oil changed in our cars every three thousand miles or with the new synthetic oils every 7-10 thousand miles. Growing up I remember always hearing the words, "as long as you maintain and service your car regularly it will run forever!" Maintaining your vehicle like that will guarantee greater performance and longer life. The same goes for our brains. The same goes for our bodies. The same goes for our peace of mind!

So why have we not put this into practice in our own lives? All these examples we know? We understand the concept of taking care of our tools, cars and sharpening our knives. Why then do we not take the time and opportunity to do this for ourselves? Our brains, bodies, emotional growth, social and physical development, intellectual growth and spirituality are in essence tools that need to be taken care of. Nurturing these can produce the most amazing results. You will be stunned at what can happen with a little effort and concentration on your part.

As an emotional intelligence expert practitioner, it is my passion to help us all grow in every way possible, including myself. The beginning of all growth comes with something we know as "self awareness".

Self-awareness is a very simple concept of being aware of what is going on both physically and mentally within. Being self aware and in the moment to recognize things that happening with in us is difficult to put into practice, thus, this book has been written to help us along the road!

There Is Nothing New Under The Sun

> *Ecclesiastes 1:9-14 NIV: what has been will be again, what has been done will be done again; there is nothing new under the sun. Is there anything of which one can say, "look!" this is something new"? It was here already, long ago; it was here before our time.*

How many times have we read self help books, leadership books, articles intended to give us tips and tricks to live a more productive and wholesome life? I am a sucker for things like that. I would go to any conference I could get my credit card to pay for! I even hitchhiked to a conference in Oklahoma once because I wanted to go so badly and had no transportation.

Deborah R. Monroe

The truth for me is that yes, I did get something out of these conferences. I did get a great deal of knowledge and information. The problem I had was that I didn't do a great deal with it when I got back to the job or home. And, if I did, the learning never seemed to stick and become a pattern. I never benefited fully from the experience in being able to intrinsically maintain the change I wanted to make. It confounded me; it frustrated me to no end. Why could I not keep this vital change in the front of my mind and take advantage of it?

I needed this information to become revelation and for the revelation to become life-formation.

I studied habits; I studied addictions, trying to understand that if one could be addicted to things that destroyed, certainly they could be addicted to things that brought life. I studied adult learning theory, how do we as adults learn? What makes us accept certain things and ignore others into our stream of every day life? I studied organizational behavior, trying to figure out what initiates and prompts a change. I read the books, I went to the conferences, I got motivated and then after 3 months it is as if I spent all the money in vane. Maybe your experience is not exactly like that, yet I know we all suffer from the same thing, and that is being human; with all our foibles, eccentricities and brains that sometimes cooperate and sometimes do not.

What I can tell you is that in being human, we all have the equivalent experience; normal brains are similarly wired; the reaction experiences of chemicals flooding our cognitive mind and our bodies occurs in each of us. Some of us are more willful than others; others are more tormented. But, in the end we all have the same tools and machinery to live here on the planet. It is how we use them, and how we decide to grow, that makes the difference within ourselves and the world that we live in.

It's All In The Delivery And Application

> *"The measure of success is not whether you have a tough problem to deal with, but whether it's the same problem you had last year."* — John Foster Dulles

So what works? Some people are ready for change and growth and some are not. If you bought this book, more than likely you are tired of the "same old same old" and ready to kick yourself into gear. You are ready to take on the challenge and be a courageous warrior. You want to sharpen that blade, clean up your tools and begin to learn how to use them more effectively.

As an emotional intelligence coach and human motivator, I have been blessed to share these tools with hundreds of individuals Over thousands of hours of coaching during the last 10 years. Over the last 20 years the influence of speaking and teaching to thousands upon thousands of individuals has given me insight into what is important to make and keep the change. It is not easy! Yet with guidance and accountability what you want to change can and will change!

You will find that this book is brief. There are many reasons behind that.

- We all have limited time and want to make the most of it

- Less is often more. Simple stories, application and accountability. Executive summary means a quick view and understanding of the content and how to apply it. If you wish to expound on the details there is a great deal of valuable material out there by many authors. Some of their resources I will recommend at the end of this book.

- Change comes by doing, rarely by simply reading. So this is your chance and challenge for change. I have developed a method that will keep you motivated, moving and growing, if you make the choice to do it.

You are the only one who will take care of yourself. No one else can make those changes. Yet, with the tools here within, you will be begin to turn your skills into art and then build the most amazing changes that will please not only you, but also your work family and your relationships outside the office.

Now let's get down to it and make it happen!

Deborah R. Monroe

How To Use This Guide

> *"To live is to choose. But to choose well, you must know who you are and what you stand for, where you want to go and why you want to get there."* Kofi Annan

The premise of this workbook is to keep you involved and alive, aware and motivated to make the little changes that will provide you with big results. Some of the topics you may already have a handle on, some you will have to put some energy into. This is a book that if applied and paid attention to, will take you 11 months to complete; eleven easy months. It is not a book to be read or flipped through all at once and then put on the shelf, saying, "Well, that was nice". That would not serve you well and it would disappoint my intention.

You can use this book one of two different ways:

1. As an individual with support from an accountability partner or coach: You can also use this as a program with your existing coach. They will use it to guide you and work with you on specific areas of improvement and growth.

2. As a group of you and your peers, team or others: You will have lively discussions once or twice a month about what you are doing and how the content and exercises helped each of you as individuals and a group. This is a great team building opportunity.

How you choose to use this is up to you! As long as you dedicate the time to yourself and sharpen your blades, you will succeed!

Every month's **BLADE** will build upon one another like learning math. It is important for us to learn how to add and subtract before we can even engage the thought of doing calculus. We will review, check successes, and offer opportunities to back track if the prior month's lesson wasn't as fruitful as you would have liked. So first things first; you can do this right now or when you get back to the office.

Go to your time management software (ms outlook or lotus notes, etc.)

1. Schedule one (1) reoccurring appointment once a month for 11 months called "**Sharpen My Blade**". The appointment will be 1.5 hours long. You will use this appointment to read your monthly chapter and any other subject matter that will help you continue your growth around the competency of that month.

2. Schedule another reoccurring appointment 2 days after your *"sharpen my blade"* appointment. Once a month for 10 months you will have an appointment called **"Clean My Tools"**. This appointment with yourself will give you the opportunity to reflect on and answer the questions at the back of each chapter. This appointment will be one (1) hour long

3. Set one more appointment for 20 minutes at the end of each month for "**Maintenance**". The intention of this appointment on your calendar is to give yourself the opportunity to reflect on how you did with each section's subject. You will spend 20 minutes filling out the log at the back of each chapter.

4. To ensure you take all this seriously, you will want to locate a coach or accountability partner for yourself; one who will serve you in the areas that you want to "sharpen". When you have chosen a coach or accountability partner, reserve two (2) fifty-minute slots on your calendar with that person to keep yourself accountable to the changes you want to make.

In total, this is a commitment to YOU. All in all, it includes coaching time, of only **4 hours and 20 minutes a month**. Out of a possible 12 hours a day or 336 hours in a month, this is time well spent on you!

Important: Make the appointments with yourself. Invest the time you need to keep promises to yourself. If you cannot keep promises to yourself, how can you keep them for anyone else?

If there is an emergency, then obviously, move the appointment as close as you can to the original. If not an emergency, then schedule time you spend with others, in meetings, at events and on projects **around** the " YOUR appointments". Make yourself the priority here.

If you find that you are moving the self-appointments to make room for other things....stop the clock! You are off track. You want to honor yourself and the commitments to yourself.

I love what **Albert Einstein** said, *"Insanity is doing the same thing over and over again and expecting different results.*

So let's make it different this time and make sure the change happens. Only you can make the choice to do that! Give yourself the time. Make room for yourself and the improvements you want to make will make room for you!

Each section will illustrate a concentration or competency with true stories, case studies, experience and researched fact. As always, names are changed to protect the guilty.

The power of this workbook, when used diligently, self-awareness of the subjects studied and applied will increase dramatically. Once self-awareness is raised, our actions and reactions become more conscious. Patterns begin to change. The way we think and ultimately the way we act is influenced, causing, the stifled behavior to change and transformation is the result.

This tool will help you *"level the playing field"* and give you the advantage that may be lacking in your personal or working environment. You will learn how to be true to yourself, tell the truth with grace, understand others' motivations, truly listen, truly hear another human being, be honest when you need to be, and remind yourself that your are an all encompassing human being, NOT a human doing. All these things reduce stress, clear our minds, and cause us to waste less time making us more productive and in a sense, creating a kinder and gentler environment for ourselves and others. The result? We create greater productivity and creativity in our lives…and who wouldn't want that?

I do want to acknowledge Mr. Stephen Covey for so brilliantly coining the phrase and bringing the woodcutter's dilemma of using a dull blade in his book, **7 *Habits Of Highly Effective People***.

Mr. Covey's 7th Habit, *Sharpen the Saw,* in summary expresses the concept of caring for one's self; giving yourself time and creating energy as you rest, generating other interests and connecting with people on a deep level. *The woodcutter's dilemma is a simple story of a man chopping down a tree for hours. A traveler passes him and asks, "how long have you been chopping at that tree"? The woodcutter replies, " a long time". The traveler asks, "Why don't you sharpen your saw"? The woodcutter says, "I don't have time". The moral of the story is plane...take time to sharpen your saw and you will be done with the job at hand in no time!*

There are many different saws for different types of cutting, like manual saws and power saws, saws to cut down branches, saws that need two people to execute a cut and saws that require one hand for operation. We have reciprocating saws, band saws, and circular saws, cross cut saws, rip saws, hacksaws, jig saws, saber saws, table saws, rotary saws, and the like. Each saw has a specific type of blade with different hardness and number of teeth. Each saw has a specific purpose and cuts wood, metal, composite, concrete, rock, tile or even Styrofoam! So there are many types of knives as well: utility knives, paring knives, boning knives, carving knives and bread knives, etc. Each one, again, has a specific purpose and makes the job you are doing easier if you have the right blade or tool for that job.

We will view each of the sections in this workbook as a specific blade for the tool for a specific type of job. Having the right tool for the right job will make your efforts in accomplishing that job much easier. It takes time and effort to sharpen a blade as well; the correct angle and sharpening implement; steel against steel, iron sharpening iron. We can consider that during our work here, you butt up against different sharpening implements too! Some of those implements may be your own thoughts, some will be patterns of behavior you have been using for many years, other implements may be people and their habits and even your accountability coach, yet whatever is used to refine these blades within you, allow them to be used upon you with gratefulness and understanding. In this you will realize your full potential beyond what I could share with you. Make yourself sharp and see how easy it will be for you to be used in service!

BLADE #1

Honor Myself

Letting the self emerge is the primary task of leaders.
— *Warren Bennis*

One of the primary things that most of us struggle with is taking care of ourselves. We don't take the time we need to improve ourselves, eat well, sleep enough or turn our brains off. We choose to serve others over ourselves. Which is noble, don't get me wrong! Yet, if we do that, in sacrificing ourselves, we end up as shells with nothing more to give. That does not serve you, your family or your job/company at all.

In this section we will spend time looking at how little changes can make a huge difference in our overall view of ourselves and how we treat others and how we treat and care for ourselves. Here is a perfect example in an article I wrote not so long ago for coaches:

When it comes to coaching, you never know which direction your client will take you and how much life circumstances affect our emotional intelligence. Consider Peter...

Peter came to me with a problem. He was considered to be very controlling and would burst with anger at the slightest aggravation. No doubt, his resilience and flexibility were stripped. Peter regularly had morning meetings at 10 o'clock with his team. He would go in hopeful and then in an hour everyone, including himself would walk out dejected and angry.

Peter and I spoke for a while and he had no idea why he lost his temper every morning with his team. "Why couldn't they do anything right?" He said.

It is important for us to know the principle of the HALT'ed state. We are more susceptible to Amygdala hijacks when we are:

(H)ungry
(A)ngry
(L)onely
(T)ired

I asked Peter if he had breakfast every morning. In fact, he didn't eat until 1 or 2 in the afternoon! He only drank coffee and did not sleep more than 5 hours a night. In a very personal conversation he also brought up his shame for being so over weight.

With the simplest things, we can get the greatest results. Peter's work between our sessions was to add 15 minutes of sleep on each end of his sleep pattern, begin to drink 3 bottles of water a day and most importantly, start small with a yogurt or power bar on the way into work. Peter also decided to throw a handful of almonds into his system 15 minutes before that morning meeting.

As coaches we listen to content that most people would consider trivial and we can "see" the more subtle issues by listening to tone of voice and language. After all it is out of the heart that the mouth speaks!

So, Peter, after practicing these small steps made huge leaps forward. Instead of "eating" his team for breakfast, he actually started eating breakfast, caring for himself and became more self-aware when he entered his HALT'ed state.

His team responded with less fear and more creativity. Now, when leaving the meeting room, conversation was flowing, critical thinking and problem solving were running as well oiled gears. An increased combination of self-regard and self-awareness, two areas that we rarely view as important, made all the difference for this director, his team and his business! Taking care of you takes care of everyone around you.

The first thing Peter had to do was to be honest with himself."

Even If It Makes Your Toes Curl Under, Be Honest With Yourself

> *"Honesty is such a lonely word, every one is so untrue; honesty is hardly ever heard and mostly what I need from you!"*
> — *Billy Joel*

Many of us won't admit that we are just not being honest with ourselves. Honesty? With myself? This is where true growth happens! This is where the proverbial rubber meets the road. It is one of the hardest things to do; just the act of thinking about change creates change; some of the change is painful. Being honest with ourselves causes us to rearrange life. Fear must be shoved in the back like an old coat in a closet. It requires us to examine our motives, our thinking, our judgments, and our relationships.

We ask these questions:

> Do I like what I do?
> Am I happy?
> Do I deserve to be happy?
> Is the price I am paying too much to bear?
> What is my motivation for doing what I do?

You have will have an opportunity to answer all these questions at the end of this section.

I heard someone say that it was easier to lie than to tell the truth. This is such a profound statement. When we lie; when we don't say what we really feel; when we don't speak up, we allow the cowering child within us who is fearful and ready for punishment to rule our lives.

It takes courage, tenacity and guts to tell the truth. The truth remains and is told by those who can take this responsibility onto their shoulders. They honor themselves and others with the valiant heart of a king when the truth is told.

Part of self-regard is being honest with ourselves. It is an important factor in emotional intelligence. Unconscious reactions affect our self-esteem… it is difficult to appear confident when you are not telling the truth to yourself. There is a splitting on the inside of us, tearing apart of the heart and mind. Again, this is probably the most difficult decision to make, these questions are the most difficult to ask, and a valiant heart is required to make the changes required once honesty has been revealed. If you doubt you have an issue with this…you may be lying to yourself!

In 2005 I went to the doctor. I was very overweight and after the doctor ran some blood work she said that I had elevated blood proteins and very high cholesterol, which if I didn't do something about would seriously impact my health. You must understand that I have always been a "larger" person based on family genetics, sport mania in my youth and Breyers ice cream. It didn't help that my father went to cooking school in Paris when we lived in Europe and I was a growing teen!

My doctor of course, was a very small woman in stature and in size. Let me tell you when a women like that tells a women like me, that we need to exercise and lose weight it can be received in an unpleasant manner! Doc was very stern in her delivery. My response went something like this, "yeah, doc, but, I am running a business, traveling all the time, I am building a house, and I don't have a partner to help me do all this. I don't have time to exercise on a regular basis"…which was my truth!

Her response almost threw me over the edge…in fact, had I not controlled my temper I would have picked her up and easily tossed her across the room, which I was fully capable of since she was so small! She said, "Deborah, even Condoleezza Rice has time to exercise an hour every day and she is busier than all of us, don't you think?" With face red and jaw tight my simple reply, was, "I guess so."

I walked out of doc's office in flurry. How the heck could she compare my life with Ms. Rice's? What a skinny b#*ch, I thought. Her words scorched my heart for two days as I sat full of pride in front of the television for hours at a time.

After a couple of days, the anger subsided and was replaced with embarrassment. Ouch, I felt really shamed. The doc was right. I had to be honest with myself. If Condoleezza Rice had the time, certainly, I had the time to exercise. What were my choices? Continue on the path that I was on and certainly die early or get my butt out of bed at 6am and take an hour for myself before the madness of the day begins.

The hardest part about the whole adventure was not getting up early; it was about being truthful with myself about what I had let happen to my body. It was overcoming the pride and realizing that no one else could fix this but me. No excuses: no blaming the stress of life, building a house, running a business, lost relationships…it was all me. Lesson learned.

What is it that you are defending inside of your own heart? The key word here is "defending". If you find yourself protecting your position, responding in that way to something someone said to you or your lifestyle, perhaps you are blaming others for your spot in life or in the job. Please take a closer look at that part of your life. More than likely, you will find, that there is no one else to blame. We can step out of being a victim to circumstances, stand up and say…no, I need to make this change with my job, my family, my housing, and my life! Just be honest with yourself…there is freedom and liberty at the end of that. For me there was a 50lb weight loss. Yes, there is still more to go, yet I know I am the one responsible for it and my choices are my choices, no one else's.

Sleep, Eat, Play, Crash And Don't Forget To Laugh

Sleep

One of the most interesting responses in my life as a facilitator is when I ask people to get a good 7 hours of sleep before they come back for class. The room fills with "ugh, no way"; "never happen", "are you insane?", "I never get more than 5 hours of sleep a night, so that is not going to happen!" Since this request is usually at the end of the day, I don't get to tell them a great deal about the science and benefits behind sleep. What seems to make the biggest impression is when I compare sleep to the workings of your computer. Everyone knows what happens when you leave computers on all the time and do not restart them.

So what does happen to the computer when we don't turn it off at the end of the day? Well, let's see, it begins to slow down. The ram is full to capacity, it takes forever to open an application and the end result is that the computer will crash and you will end up restarting and perhaps, will have lost some of your data. Your brain needs to be turned off and a good sleep with plenty of REM state sleep does just that. There is so much science out there about this subject that I don't have enough time to fill you in completely, except:

According to the National Sleep Foundation if you don't get enough sleep, expect this:

- Increased risk of motor vehicle accidents

- Increase in body mass index – a greater likelihood of obesity due to an increased in appetite caused by sleep deprivation

- Increased risk of diabetes and heart problems

- Increased risk for psychiatric conditions including depression and substance abuse

- Decreased ability to pay attention, react to signals or remember new information

Experts say that an adult should be sleeping between 8-10 hours a night and children between 10-12 hours a night for optimal performance and health. Adults need their circadian rhythm to run between 10pm and 6 am for optimum health and performance.

I know your response might be, that there is no way in heaven that this will happen, not with all that I have going on in my life!

Yet, perhaps the reason we have so much going on in our lives is because we are spending much too much time resolving problems and working. As a result, we are not being as productive and creative as we can be because we are not getting enough sleep!

So the challenge at the end of this chapter for you will be to add 15 minutes to the beginning of your sleep cycle and 15 minutes to the end of the sleep cycle. Remember, tiny consistent changes make the biggest difference!

Eat

Yes, this is something that I struggle with. I don't have a problem eating; it is what I eat and when I eat that creates the problem!

Let's look at Peter; one of his biggest issues was that he did not eat breakfast. Instead of eating breakfast he ate his team instead! The challenge was to put some kind of protein bar or banana in his car to have some type of nourishment before he went into work. One of the other things we challenged Peter with was to bring a handful of almonds and eat them before he went into a meeting. The simple change in his diet made a complex and immediate change in his wellbeing, in his weight loss and for his team and his management style.

Skipping meals is not healthy. "I don't have time to eat", is not a good excuse either. We now know that eating several small meals a day is the optimum way to keep our metabolism up, our brain functioning at its best and our body fed with the fuel it needs to perform at its peak.

Keep healthy food handy at work, so you are not tempted to munch on garbage in the mid afternoon.

Another thing to remind you, is that when we are hungry, we are more vulnerable to emotional upset and what we in the emotional intelligence world, call an Amygdala hijack. Our fight, flight or freeze mechanism triggers much more readily when hungry. I come from a family of 'grumpies". When we don't eat we all get crabby and short tempered. Now that we all know this, we try not to talk to one another when we are "low on sugar" or we pay for the results in apologies!

Exercise

I know, I know…I just told you my story about exercise…you already know how important it is and you have been preached to enough by every television program, doctor and book you can lay your hands on. So I simply want to encourage you and myself by saying again, *small incremental consistent changes make the biggest difference.*

When I began my exercise routine, the only thing I could seriously commit to was walking down the end of the road and back on Monday, Wednesday and Friday. That was all. 15 minutes three times a week was my big commitment. Soon, I did a mile, then 2 miles, then 3 miles. Then I was walking 4, 5, and 6 times a week. Sometimes I did the 3 miles twice a day. My inner chemistry changed. I felt good, finally.

So, in between that time and now, I completely stopped all that healthy walking. It seems that when we need it the most, is when we do it the least. Yet, it is my decision and I realize that. So when faced recently with a choice of Christmas presents, instead of choosing the wonderful gift of top-of-the-line pots and pans for cooking the most magnificent meals I could prepare, with rich buttery wine filled sauces, I chose an elliptical trainer instead.

Once again, Dad's wisdom shining through; while in his fifties, he said to me, "Start exercising now and taking care of yourself now so that you can be in great shape by the time you get to be my age, otherwise you will pay for it later." I really didn't take what he said to heart at the time, few words spoken in wisdom ever are! Well, just before Dad's 70th birthday he went mountain biking in the Himalayas for 3 weeks. He muscled his way through the thin air, up and down the primitive roads…while I become winded with the simple act of climbing stairs…

I feel good about the choice I made; the choice to make myself healthy and stronger. If you are already doing this, then God bless you! If not, let's make the choice to do something small and consistent together.

Crash and Laugh

Everybody needs a crash day. When was the last time you actually gave yourself permission to have one? Of course, it helps if you know what a *crash day* is! So here is my definition:

A *Crash Day* is a day where we put aside all the "I have to's", "I need to's and "I should do's". It is the day that the "I want to's" and the "I love to's" reign.

When you begin to make room for a crash day in your schedule once a month you will want to give yourself permission, otherwise guilt will eat you up like a hungry dog. When I say, give yourself permission, I mean, to actually speak to yourself! "Deborah, I give you permission to take a crash day." You may have to say it several times the first time you do it or you may end up doing one of the "I really need to" things out of guilt. We will talk more about this in a later chapter, yet for now, put it on your radar as a good thing to practice, for the benefits of doing this will make you human again.

Here's what happened to me when I didn't take my own advice:

After traveling the whole week, instead of crashing on Saturday, which is my custom, I got caught up in one of the "I need to's" in my life. I went to a large superstore to return an item. Although it was early in the morning the line at the return counter was 10-people deep. The clerk at the counter was, in my estimation, slow and having a pleasant conversation about a local football game with their current customer. After 5 minutes and limited movement I was getting a little perturbed. I looked around and saw several other employees meandering down the way, laughing and sharing with no care of getting to work. I could feel the blood rising in my face and looked at the clock. The frustration was felt in the tightening of my jaw and when my nostrils began to flare I knew someone was in line to get a verbal whipping.

I politely asked the person behind me, who had been complaining, to hold my place in line while I found a manager that could help with the situation and provide another person behind the return counter. I boldly strode out of line and found someone in the "manager box" near the cash registers. With eyes ablaze, voice firm and diction crisp and slow, I stated my case. "Will, you PLEASE find someone to work behind the return counter; we have been standing in the same place forever." Without thought the woman blankly stared at me and said, "Well, Mam, there is nothing I can do." "Excuse me? There is nothing you can do? That is not acceptable." I stated like a two year old about to have a temper tantrum. "Mam, this is my first day and…" "I don't care if this is your first day or not, find someone and get them behind that return counter". Storming off, I thought, what an idiot, who the heck uses "this is my first day on the job" as an excuse?

I was soon back in the return line and approached by a manager. She probably knew to come to me because I was the one with my head on fire. I stated my case again with direct fervor and in addition, railed at the manager for not having the proper training in place for new people, especially if they were going to reply to every request with "It's my first day on the job". What a poor job they were doing with their training.

After another 15 minutes in line I finished my business and left the store. What I took with me was a sense that I had really blown it. I was ashamed of my behavior and very embarrassed. I argued with myself in the car, slammed the door and walked back into the superstore knowing that I needed to apologize to the poor lady I had attacked. I waited around her register like a stalker until she had no one in her line. "Mam", I said, "Please forgive me, I was not frustrated with you, I was frustrated with the situation and the fact that this company didn't give you the tools that you need to answer questions. I am so sorry for my behavior."

The woman reached out for my hand and with tears in both of our eyes, she thanked me and said that was the nicest thing someone had done for her in a long time. I walked away scolding myself for not staying home that morning! I also walked away humbled, glad that I faced my bad behavior and myself.

This more than likely never would have happened had I taken my crash time and stayed away from public places. I knew my resilience was low. I knew that after a week on the road I was not ready for what I call, "Human Consumption". I know myself and I did myself and another person a disservice. Considering what I have told you here, can you see when you are stretched beyond capacity and ready to snap? Take my lesson and apply it to yourself; if you know that you are at the edge, give yourself a break and give those around you the break as well. It is better to allow yourself to regenerate than to pour out what is left like a bottle of sour milk! And, if you ever see me in a store on a Saturday morning, come up to me and tell me to go home--do us both a favor!

Laugh

Laugh a whole lot. Find someone who makes you laugh and bother the heck out of them. We know that laughter heals the soul. We know that it heals the bones. We know that laughter increases endorphins and releases stress. Find a humor conference, listen to stand up comedy, read Dave

Barry books; if clowns don't scare you, become one! Whatever it takes, laugh…as long as it is not at someone else's expense.

You know you can be a catalyst for laughter. All you need to do is start laughing, even if you don't feel like it! Simply start out with laughing to yourself…hee hee hee, ho ho ho, ha ha ha over and over again. Once the pump is primed, you will find it hysterically easy to "ROFL" (roll on the floor laughing). We know that emotion is contagious, in fact it is viral. I know this sounds strange…however, when you do it, you fill find it works and your mood with change!

The American Journal of Cardiology 11/2003 stated this:

"Electrophysiological changes in feelings are conveyed by the heart's electrical field and can be felt and measured up to 10 feet away."

Daniel Goleman makes more proof of that in the book Primal Leadership. In essence the leader's emotions spread though an organization. We know this to be true when we want to go speak to our managers. We walk past their office and instantly know if it is a good day or a bad day to approach them.

So use your power for good, not for evil! Change your world and the world of others with laughter!

Clean My Tools

> *"Leaders must be as willing to be transformed as they are to transform others."* — Glenda Eoyang

This section was all about you. We need to begin at the beginning and the beginning is you; honoring yourself, regarding yourself, being true to yourself, being honest with yourself, taking care of yourself. In doing these things, you can and will be in better functioning shape to deal with the issues and people around you.

As I read this section, what was it that impacted me? What can I begin to do for myself?

_____

_____

_____

What can I implement as a small incremental consistent change today?

_____

_____

_____

Do I need extra sleep? How can I add 15 minutes to each end of my sleep?

_____

_____

What food do I need to bring into the office to keep my brain and body working at their prime?

How can I change my eating habits to more effectively fuel my body and when am I going to start?

Am I exercising enough? If not, what can I do that makes me happy and gets me moving? When will I begin? Who is going to keep me accountable?

Go to the calendar and schedule some crash time once a month for a half-day to begin with. Make it a reoccurring appointment.

If I have a significant other, what can I do to encourage their crash day once a month?

What do I honestly need to look at within myself that I may be hiding? What do I get defensive about when people bring the subject up? What is my next step in bringing that into the light and dealing with it?

How can I laugh more? What is funny to me? Can I commit to laughing at least three times a day?

Do I like what I do? If not why not?

Am I happy? Why or why not?

Do I deserve to be happy? Why?

Deborah R. Monroe

Is the price I am paying too much to endure? If it is what needs to change?

What is my motivation for doing what I do? What is driving me?

Maintenance

> *"Knowing others is intelligence; knowing yourself is true wisdom."* — Tao Te Ching

Over the last month, what did I implement and start the change process?

Sleep

Eating

Exercise

Crash time

Laughter

How am I feeling now that I have begun to implement these small consistent changes?

_____

_____

_____

What differences have I seen in my own behavior? What have others begun to see?

_____

_____

Deborah R. Monroe

Which change has made the biggest difference for me?

Is there anything in which I want to increase commitment?

BLADE #2

Manage My Distractions

"Today I felt like a fat man going through trenches, I got stuck every time I turned around" — *Joseph Pippin*

Yes, I know that this quote is not quite *politically correct*. But before you burn me at the stake, hear me and hear the context.

If you have not already gathered, I am a road warrior. I travel a great deal. This is a lonely life on the road. One of the things that make the travel manageable is the people that I meet along the way. Recently I was stuck in Houston over night due to weather issues. I found a room at the local airport hotel and headed up to the bar/restaurant for a late night light dinner and human interaction. The other alternative was to watch television in the hotel room alone or walk aimlessly through the airport, and neither of those grabbed my interest.

While eating and "trying" to read my new **David Rock** book, "***Your Brain At Work***", I was aggravated by the very loud music playing and the pulsing beat drove me to distraction. A couple of louder voices laughing and shouting at the bar caused my brows to furrow. I put pieces of a rolled up napkin in my ears to stop the insanity around me. I begin to get very annoyed at the whole experience. When I had had enough, I took my bill up to the waitress, next to the rabble-rousers. I gave them a tired smile and said, "How was your day", with thoughts of "The least I can do is be nice, they are after all, having a wonderful time, even if I am not".

A jovial Joseph with a coy smile turned to me and with a thick Louisiana accent merrily stated, *"My day? Well, today I felt like a fat man going through trenches, I got stuck every time I turned around"*!

I burst into laughter. How could I not? It is a practice in the Southern part of the United States to produce all kinds of amazing, and perhaps inappropriate metaphors or analogies by which we compare circumstances or describe experiences. Now I share all this, because as I thought about what Joseph had said, I saw a great deal of truth in it, especially for this section.

The truth or principle here is that we get "fat" with too much to do, overwhelmed with tasks, life, events, etc., and end up getting stuck every time we turn around. Our brain can handle only so much before smoke begins coming out of our ears. It is a scientific fact (not the smoke coming out of our ears, but the brain becoming overwhelmed)!

The wonderful author and brilliant leadership mentor, David Rock gives us a great view in his book, **Your Brain At Work,** of all of the things going on in our brain as props, actors, and directors on a stage. If indeed, there is too much activity on that stage, chaos ensues and the play falls apart. This is what happens to us on a daily basis. We are too fat with stuff to do.

According to Charlie Greer of the National Science Foundation the average person thinks about twelve thousand (12,000) thoughts per day. A deeper thinker can have as many as fifty thousand (50,000) thoughts daily. Deepak Chopra says that 95% of those thoughts are the same. The "don't forget to pick up the milk after work", type of thoughts.

I want to impress upon you the importance of managing distractions. If you do not manage the distractions, the distractions will manage you. Distractions come in all different forms. There are time distracters, emotional distracters, and financial distracters to name a few. I will not write a time management book here, as there are so many that have already been written and are well worth the read and application. What I will talk to you about are the main elements that I use to teach in my courses, to coach my executives on a consistent basis and some things that have changed my life when it comes to managing my time and brain energy.

Earlier, we talked about the brain being very much like a computer. The brain's working memory acts like a computer's RAM. The more applications that are open in a computer, the more that it needs to access those programs at any given time, the slower the computer will run, no matter how much RAM you have inside of that computer.

I will give you three things here in this section that will begin to change your life once you implement them. These are the best of the best; the top three life changers for managing distractions and time. Are you ready? Don't laugh, just do them and watch your life change!

1. Do a brain dump

2. Empty your inbox

3. Inhibit your mobile device!

Who knew it could be so easy! Here is the reasoning behind it all.

Deborah R. Monroe

Do a Brain Dump

No doubt, like me, you love to read and learn new techniques about how to manage your life and time. I am almost embarrassed at how much time I have put into learning how to manage my time and priorities. Looking back it seems like a "waste of time"! I remember back in the late 1980's and early 1990's, I invested in a big scheduling book and took a five-day class from 8am to 6pm to learn how to use it. I also must have spent around $1500 or more for that week of training. To be honest, I spent most of my time lying on a bunch of chairs in the back of the room wanting to poke my eyes out because of the boredom.

The course I attended was obviously designed for the detail-oriented learner in mind, of which I am not even close. I did however, succumb to following the rules and even more exhilarating for me was the opportunity to have my own, "duel color pig suede embossed, engraved important looking, don't bother me, because, can't you see how important I am, can't run my life without it, seven pound accessorized to the hilt life management holy companion". For which, I opened and used at every opportunity, carried with me to every meeting and proudly stated when speaking to a colleague, "Oh, wait, let me get my "Daytimer". The sad thing is that now I have people in my courses that have no clue about what a "Daytimer" is. I have not used it in 13 years, yet, I cannot emotionally muster myself to throw it out. It still looks as good as it did the day I bought it. My name still shines in the bottom right hand corner. I know I will never use it again, but it holds so many memories!

The next generation of time management philosophy that went wild on us was namely, to place our time into our priorities. Where you heart or priority is, that is where you will spend your time. I explain in my time management courses, that this concept gave me full authorization to go out and hire a house cleaner! You see, in that instance, after traveling all week for work the last thing I wanted to do when I got home was spend 4 hours cleaning my house. I am neither good at it nor like to do it. For a female, that is a very difficult submission and confession based upon social morays and demands.

The problem with my situation is that although I don't like cleaning and I am not good at it, I absolutely love a clean house. I would rather spend my time with my nephew, hanging out, going for a walk, exploring a cave, and laughing at silly jokes. With that in mind, my priority is my nephew, not cleaning my house. If I am to spend time in my priority, I am to spend it elsewhere and "outsource" the other job, thus a house cleaner! Makes perfect sense to me! As it should you!

The issue with this time management idea for me was and is that everything is a priority, whether I like it or not and I could only outsource or delegate so much before people would start to look at me with funny expressions on their faces. I became overwhelmed and burned out.

I then went to a class on "managing multiple priorities" and became more confused. I once fell upon **David Allen's** time book, *Getting Things Done*. It was long and detailed. The changes he asked me to make were arduous and contradicted much of my previous learning. This does not mean that it was bad information or that it was ineffective. I look at resources like this book in one way, if I can take one or two things away that will improve my life and make me better, and then the whole experience is well worth it.

This is what I got from David Allen that changed my life.

Think of your brain as a computer, once again. Too many applications, and too many programs open on a computer slow down the machine. If you have too many things running around in your working memory and short-term memory, you are constantly trying to remember them so that you don't forget to do them. That is the nature of the beast.

With all this information clogging up the works in the brain, the brain reacts by being unable to focus, be creative, or problem solve and typically becomes slower in all reactions and interactions. David Allen said, "Write it all down", meaning, he wanted me to do a data dump! And a data dump, I did…

I just began to write down all the things that I was keeping in my head; projects I wanted to do in the future, things that needed to be done around the house, items that needed to be picked up at the hardware store, people I wanted to call or send an email to. Every thing I could possibly think of.

The list was unbelievably long. Then, when I thought I was finished, I would take a break and 5 more things would pop up in my mind. I would run back upstairs and write them down. I would go to bed and more of the "clog" would spin to the top of my mind. At first, I would get up and go back into the office and begin writing, until I had the brilliant idea of putting a notepad next to my bed with a flashlight. By the time I finished the brain dump I had over 450 items on paper. I could hardly believe that I had been holding all this in my working memory. No wonder I could not focus. No wonder I was unproductive in my work and home tasks. Yet, the dump was complete for the moment.

David Allen then suggested separating things on the list. The most useful information for me was to take anything that could be done in less than two minutes and actually do it. I went down the 450-item list I had created and color-coded everything I could do in two minutes. The next day, I was able to get over 50 of the items completed. It was in all estimation, a true miracle.

I keep to this philosophy to this day. I keep my head clear of "need to's, have to's and should do's". And, if I can do anything in two minutes or less, I just do them. The results for me have been incredible. My mind is clearer, my focus crisper and my life less complicated.

I will challenge you this month to do a "brain dump" it will take you longer than the scheduled hour to complete the "Clean My Tools" section. Yet, in every way, it will be totally worth it for your mental health and brain function.

Empty Your Inbox

Email distracts all day long. That little beep or flash on the bottom of your screen as it floats from server to server ends up grabbing your coat sleeve like a child in need and pulls you in a thousand different directions.

There are several tricks to keep email at bay and they have been written about in many books of note. I will make it simple for you.

Think first about how many emails you get on average every day, most likely about 150. Now let's think about the time given on average to each email, around 3 minutes. Some you just delete, some you spend 20 minutes on, and so 3 minutes is a good average. Now let's do the math. 150 times 3 equal 450 minutes. Divide that by 60 minutes. That means that in some way shape or form you are doing about 7 hours of email every day.

How do we expect to get anything done if concentrating on email is the majority of what we are doing? There is no way we can focus on building strategies to help our business grow. There is no way that we can coach and mentor our teams, or even create a valuable team environment if all we are doing is going to meetings and working on emails.

What happens here is that something is going to suffer. More than likely it will be your work itself and your staff. Because we cannot give 7 hours a day to email in the office, we end up letting our inboxes fill up to overflowing. Some executives that I work with started this process with me with over 7000 emails in their inbox! There is absolutely no way that we can keep track of that. The burden of all those emails does wear on us, creates stress and tires us out simply thinking about it.

I do want to encourage you. There is a way to get out of the pit. There is a way to keep out of the pit. So here are a couple of items [tips?] to guide you. It can be done! It has been done and you can do it! I did and so have most of the people I have had the opportunity to speak to and coach.

1. An Inbox is just that, it is an *IN-box*. At the end of the day, the inbox should be empty. You take things from the inbox and do one of 4 things to them.

   Delete it

   Do it (if it takes less than 2 minutes)

   Delegate it to someone else

   Defer it until later with a follow up flag

2. Really look at the email you receive and figure out which email lists you need to be on and which ones you can gracefully bow out of. Stop the madness at the source.

3. Create folders so that you can move the email you need to and want to keep. Then create rules that place emails into the folders when they arrive. You will be able to see what needs to be read in your "unread email folder".

4. Do not be overwhelmed by the task of cleaning out the inbox. One of my favorite sayings is, "How do you eat an elephant"? The answer of course, is "One bite at a time". Remember, small incremental consistent changes make a difference. Therefore, use 15 minutes a day to begin going through the backlog you have stored for the last year or two. I use the time on airplanes to do this. I also go though my sent items, as this folder needs to be cleared as well every six months. You can work up to 15 minutes in the morning and 15 minutes at the end of the day. You will be amazed at how fast your success will come by doing this.

The reward and freedom experienced by completing this challenge is exhilarating. When you finally see that white empty space with nothing calling your name at the end of the day, the result is that your head is clear and your mind is at rest. You may even be slightly *put out* when someone starts sending you email and filling that inbox up again. Keep on top of it. One or two days may go by without the ability to empty it. If that does happen, just take an extra 15 minutes the next day and take care of it.

Bonnie was an executive who I had the honor to work with and coach. Bonnie did just this. In fact, the day I suggested it her, she basically laughed in my face with "yeah, like that will ever happen"! Two weeks later, to her amazement she burst onto our coaching call with amazement that she had dumped 1500 emails in that short period of time. By the next call that inbox was totally empty. So empty in fact that she was able to go on vacation for the first time in 10 years. She assigned any incoming email to her second in command and gave that person the authority to cover 80% of the work. If they absolutely needed her to handle something, they would call her for direction.

As it turned out, she received only one call during her 10-day vacation. When she returned she had only 5 new emails in her inbox as it had all been handled by her second in command.

The inbox was the obvious small victory here. The big win was that she learned to delegate and to trust her staff. She increased their problem solving and critical thinking skills and made them feel valued and important part of the organization. From one small lesson came a leap of leadership qualities that grew an underutilized team into a functional, performing team; able to take on responsibilities that it had never thought possible.

Make this happen for yourself.

This month's exercises have taken some excess time, it is true! The only reason that happened is because we had to clean up the mess. With the mess cleaned up, you will never have to do this again! Maintenance is minimal and easy.

Inhibit Your Mobile Device

Now to an action item that will really change the life you lead and the way that people react to you. Inhibit your mobile device! Let's look at the definition of *inhibit* as given by the "free dictionary" online.

1. To hold back; restrain.

2. To prohibit; forbid.

3. *Psychology* to suppress or restrain (behavior, an impulse, or a desire) consciously or unconsciously.

4. *Chemistry* to prevent or decrease the rate of (a reaction).

    Biology to decrease, limit, or block the action or function of (an enzyme or organ, for example).

In this section we will concentrate on definitions 3 and 4. To inhibit this piece of technology is actually going to involve the psychological suppression of the impulse and desire to whip out the "crack berry"! And that, in essence, has turned into a chemical and biological need. Don't believe me? Here's what happened.

I have owned one of these devices for many years. I have a friend who even texts when he drives. First, I don't know how that is possible. That is until I started doing it myself; briefly, in small spurts. Some time last year I began to notice that when I received an email or text, the double buzz on the device caused me to stop whatever I was doing and look at the phone.

I broke eye contact with whoever I was in conversation with. I reached down to my right side, un-clipped the black messaging machine from its holder and like a gunman drawing this six shooter with seconds to spare, I pulled it from it's holster and drew it to my face while pressing the center button to activate the light. One smooth dynamic move, practiced 50 times a day. I was good at that.

I was on vacation. The foreign terrain of Iceland surrounded me, the desolate landscape reached far and wide into the horizon. I was in wonder, pondering the moment and the history of the vast and volcanic land. I was present in my experience; absorbing, sensing and being, after all, this is what being human is all about, right? Then, there it was…I felt the buzz on my hip…then another…I was drawn out of Iceland into the little black box on my belt. The email was nothing, just a note from some spammer. I looked up again to reality and realized at that moment I had a problem! I was addicted. What was worse was I had missed some spectacular geo thermal spew as the car went speeding by. I would never have the opportunity to see that moment again.

I am self aware enough to know this. I had a "Pavlovian" response! Just like Pavlov's dogs, trained to salivate at the sound of a bell, I had a visceral physical response to the buzz on my hip. That night I turned the vibrate function off and only left the option for the phone to ring. I wanted control back in my life. I got it back. Now, I am the one who is in charge of when I look at the phone and when I don't, yet it was a difficult transition.

We not only have to be concerned about our own responses to this new ruler of our behavior, but also the relationships, which can easily be affected. Those relationships, whether at work or at home can be greatly damaged as we pull our attention away from the simplest of conversations.

In mid-sentence with one of our co-workers we sleekly react to the buzz of the "device". With a smooth look, our eyes say silently, "Will you hold on a minute, while I check this"? We focus completely on the small screen in front of our face, and then briefly look up at the human being in front of us. We see that they are standing aimlessly and uncomfortably in front of us. We continue checking to see who needs us thru email, and then with the swiftness of a sword handler, we replace the phone back in the holder and continue our conversation with the human being, like nothing had ever interrupted the flow.

If I had not spent so much time working with people to help them build and improve their relationships, this one thing would not matter. Hear my heart when I say that it is nice to be needed. It is nice to feel important and seeing all those emails coming in makes us feel that way. What happens though is that those who really need us or our help, are standing in front of us. We disrespect them by thinking we are needed elsewhere in a little black mobile device.

My challenge to you is to inhibit this habit. Put it in its place. If we looked in the mirror as much as we looked at the device, people would call us conceited and full of ourselves. Now they call us disrespectful, a person who doesn't listen, doesn't care, and is totally self-absorbed by self-importance. We are the ones loosing out on the human experience. We are the ones damaging the relationships and we are the ones that can change that in an instant.

With any addiction, the first step to recovery is to admit that you have a problem! And when I say "you", I am pointing to myself as well. Take baby steps to make the changes that will impact your life. Here's what we can do together:

- Turn off the buzz on the email. Obviously, it is ok to check your email throughout the day, but don't react to every notification.

- When you are engaged in conversation, a meeting, a training class or a vacation, turn the blasted thing off or ignore (inhibit) it until your conversation, meeting, training class or vacation day is over.

- If you absolutely must look at your phone or take a call while you are having a human interaction, excuse yourself verbally, asking permission and thanking the person in front of you. Move away from them and speak on the phone softly with your "inside voice". When you return to the human you were previously speaking to, apologize and thank them again for their patience. And by the way, you do not have to tell them what the call or email was about. That remains your business.

- Arrange to have a "**technology-free**" day once a week. I have heard of some companies on the west coast that have email free Fridays, where if you want to communicate with someone, you must get out of your seat and see that person or call them on the phone. Brilliant! What a concept! Although you may not work in that type of environment, certainly you can arrange to enjoy one day a week that involves no technology at all. We will call it a "Sabbath"! A rest from the weary workweek. There is a miracle that can happen when we observe. You will find that your energy can be much improved and you are then raring to go on Monday with a greater energy and resilience. You will also find that it will bring back some of your humanness as well!

We have work to do this month, so hang in there. Be determined and we will get through it. Since you are taking better care of yourself having already done **BLADE # 1**, you will already have more energy and ability to stay focused. You are eating better and sleeping better, that in itself will be invaluable in helping us complete and apply everything that is important this month.

Clean My Tools

> *"Earlier today I asked my daughter, Anna, to clean up her mess in the family room. Not only toys, but a huge mess. She said she didn't do it (she was the only child home). So I asked her, "If you didn't make the mess, then who made it?" she said, "God". I said, "No, he didn't." she said, "Yes he did, Mommy, you said He makes everything."* — Ingrid B.'s daughter Anna

Out of the mouth of babes, speaks the wisdom of the world! According to Anna, God did make everything… except our messes! Our saving grace is that He does help us clean them up if necessary.

This month is about cleaning up messes; the messes made by our inability to manage the overwhelming influx and influence of the uncontrolled pour of stimulus that reigns down every single day of our existence. I know that sentence was very dramatic, yet still, true at the least.

Task 1: Do The Brain Dump

Go to your calendar right now and schedule **2 hours** to complete this exercise. You can do this on the train going home, at home instead of watching television or without guilt in the middle of your work day... because we will call it strategic planning! Go ahead, I will wait!

Ok, now that you are done with that we can move on.

Do the brain dump! No questions to ask or answer here in this task, just a freeing exercise. Get out a notebook or 5 sheets of paper, a fresh pen. Do not worry about categorizing the information into neat sections. Just empty your head on paper. For some reason this means more to you when you put pen to paper rather than typing it. There is a visceral completeness when creating the act of writing on paper which typing cannot possibly deliver. Besides, we could all use some practice with our handwriting skills! Write down:

1. Everything that you have been trying to remember to do.

2. Everything that you ever wanted to do.

3. Anywhere you ever dreamed of going.

4. Any books you have wanted to read or write.

5. Anything that you have been meaning to say to someone

6. Anything on the "honey-do" list that has been put off.

7. Any inventions, creative ideas, business ideas that you have been holding in your head.

8. Any regrets that you have and need to deal with.

9. Anything else you can think of that has been stuck up there for the last year or two.

You get it, right? Write it all down. Put a pad of paper by your bed and expect that you will be using it by default. Put a pad of paper in the kitchen and every time you run out of something or figure you need another item there; write it down instead of trying to remember that you need to purchase it. The act of trying to remember is what clogs the works and causes the system of our brain to slow.

Task 2: Wipe Out The 2 Minute Items

You are probably feeling light headed after finishing **Task 1.** Give yourself a couple of days away from the dumping ground. Let your mind reset itself. If more items surface, add them to the list. Please do not worry about accomplishing or categorizing the list yet. Remember, you eat an elephant one bite at a time!

1. When you are ready, schedule 30 minutes only to go through the list

2. Mark the 2-minute items. You know, the ones that will take only 2 minutes or less to complete.

3. Once those are marked off, keep the list with you at all times and if you want to categorize the 2-minute items between home and work, go for it.

4. Ready, set….go…begin to attack the 2-minute items, one at a time. They are easy! The fun part is…

5. Once you do them, cross them off the long list you have been carrying around. Oh, the feeling of saying, "this is done!" Has such finality and satisfaction. Before you know it, your list will be down to nothing.

6. I don't want to leave you with a huge list of other things, so I will suggest that you begin by appropriating **David Allen's** book, *Getting Things Done*. He will tell you what needs to happen next with the remainder of the list. He is a wise man, so listen to what he has to say!

Task 3: Clean Out Your Inbox

You are a brave soul. You can do this. I have full confidence. All you need to begin is 15 minutes a day (you choose when). Do not do more than that unless you have nothing to do on the weekend.

Cleaning out your inbox too fast would be like eating too much tiramisu in one sitting. You will not want to smell it, see it, think about it or eat it for a long time. Doing this all at once will ruin your taste for a good thing. This is the time to inhibit your desire to accomplish a task all at once. It does not need to be finished immediately. Carry on in small consistent incremental bites through the whole month. All you need to do is schedule that 15 minutes on your calendar and then do it. If you cannot begin with 5 days a week, then begin with only 2 days a week. It doesn't matter, as long as you simply begin the process.

We will check with you and your progress in the **Maintenance** part of this section later in the month. Until then…keep up the good work!

Task 4: The 4 D's

Appropriate the 4D's. Bring them into your life! Once you do the 4 D's you will add the "fifth D"…you will DANCE!

1. Watch what comes into your inbox. If you can get off the mailing list, get off the mailing list.

2. Create rules for yourself in your email management software. If you do not know how, call the support center or help desk at work and have them refer you, teach you or show you how to do it.

3. If it is not important delete it right away.

4. If you can answer, forward or do something with the email under 2 minutes, do it. Get it over with.

5. If the item is something you can delegate off your plate, then forward it on to that person with a note stating what your expectations are and when you want them to follow up with you on the details. Delegate it.

6. Lastly, if you know that email is going to take you more than two minutes to complete, flag it with a date and put it in the appropriate folder. When you put the flag on it, also put a date for your action. Or you can simply drag that email onto your calendar to make room to work on it. Defer it, schedule it and do it…

Task 5: Inhibit The Mobile Device

In some ways, you have had a great deal of change this month. If you have been able to accomplish the first four tasks, I almost want to reward you in your efforts by going out for a drink with you. If you don't drink, I want to give you a hug for your efforts instead! Don't think that you have to be perfect at all of this by the end of the month…you do not have to be perfect, all you need do is have made a start. Do be encouraged. If at first it takes a while to get up and running, that is ok, keep eating that elephant. (my apologies to the vegetarians, you do understand this is only a metaphor!)

This task is to inhibit the "device". As I sit here, I almost want to call it the "evil" device…with a grin on my face and a warning in my eye.

I can tell you what to do here, yet the change will only come as you control and resist the temptation of the addiction to check it every half hour. So here is where to begin

1. Put the ringer on "phone only".

2. When someone is talking to you, make them the only thing in the world and ignore the device.

3. When you are in a meeting or training, don't think that we can't see what you are doing under the table! Turn it off and be present, pay attention and be there…even if you are bored, you may build a relationship that will help your future.

4. Give yourself permission to check the device every 1.5 hours to start. No more! See if you can manage the self-control aspect of this exercise.

5. Unless "they" will fire you, turn the device off on Sundays and have a real life full of human beings, outdoor activities, games, food and fun.

6. Give others the respect, honor and attention that they deserve when in your presence, just as you would want to be treated. The people who need you are standing in front of you. They need your attention and relationship more than you need a relationship with a smart phone.

You are a courageous soul. You will be able to do this month's task. We will check in at the end of the month. If you need help write down what you are struggling with and then bring it with you to **Section 3.** We can deal with the remaining issues in that section.

Maintenance

> *"In the long run, we shape our lives, and we shape ourselves. The process never ends until we die. And the choices we make are ultimately our own responsibility."* — Eleanor Roosevelt

This month's section was a "biggy". Let's look at what happened.

What task(s) did you excel at this month?

_____

_____

_____

How are you feeling about your accomplishments and why?

_____

_____

If you needed help on any one thing, what would it have been?

Which task did you struggle with the most?

What type of help do you need to make the changes you want to?

Do you need an accountability partner? If so, who would that be?

Are you being honest with yourself about how you treat others or are you hiding behind the "device"?

Did you get that inbox cleared out? If not, when do you want it to be finalized?

Concerning the brain dump, what was your biggest revelation and surprise after you completed that exercise?

Have you noticed a difference in the way you feel about yourself and your accomplishments? What is different?

Has your time started to free up? If so, what percentage? What are you doing with the extra time?

Has anyone else noticed the changes you are making? Has anyone commented on how your listening skills are changing? Do people feel friendlier towards you? Make a note of what you have noticed.

BLADE #3

Get Myself A Coach

"If you look to lead, invest at least 50% of your time leading yourself." — Dee Hock

Naturally being a coach, I am an advocate of coaching. I personally have what I consider to be three (3) coaches for my growth and accountability. What I love about coaching is that the effect and affect it has on each person involved in the process. If we coach to the business side of the human being, it always influences the personal side of their lives. If you choose to work on things that are happening at home, you can bet that the beneficial effect will soon manifest in the office!

You are after all a solitary person. If you find yourself acting in two different manners…one way at work and another way at home, the congruency of your personality may be under stress.

A coach is a facilitator of self-directed neuro-plasticity, which translates to: someone can help you change your ingrained patterns of thinking. When behavior splits and we act differently in one place or another we simply endanger our core selves. If we do it long enough, we split our personality and our actions into two…and I do believe that at that point there is medication to help!!!

Think about it. Wouldn't it be nice to have someone help you solve those tender issues, either at home or at work? Someone you can count on to help you make changes or decisions. Coaches are objective. They have no agenda. Coaches' act as confidants, your experience is confidential.

Sometimes we are faced with situations that confound us. We do the best we can. Sometimes it works and sometime it doesn't. Do we really want to tell our managers about some of the issues we are facing, what will they think of us if we ask questions that put our ability in a vulnerable position? Or we risk the possibility of retribution. Even if it is not ethical, the risk remains.

It may not be appropriate to talk to our peers about some of the issues we are facing. It may be even more inappropriate to talk to our direct reports or subordinates, if we have them. Our significant others may be supportive and yet they have a tendency to be subjective in their responses. Even so, they may not understand the full depth of an issue in our offices.

Growing and be accountable in your development can be a very delicate and difficult place to be. Your coach will see patterns of behavior; they can see when you are at risk and suggest changes and applicable skills to practice. Your coach will work with you to find the motivational emotion behind the behavioral patterns that may not be serving you well any more.

All in all a coach is a good thing. I recommend finding one as soon as possible! We don't need to be judged for our behavior! Most of us know where our challenges are. What we need is support to change; someone to understand and to share wisdom and keep us accountable to make the change we want.

When picking a coach, be sure that they are an outstanding question asker. You are really seeking someone who can lead you to your own answers. You are looking for someone who you feel innately comfortable with; someone who you would not be afraid to share your deepest secrets with, knowing that there would never be a gasp on the other end of the phone. Someone who will make you question your own decisions and reactions.

Another thing to note is that a coach is not a therapist, although, there can be a thin line between therapy and coaching. Just be conscious that if it starts to get really deep, you may want to seek another type of professional help and your coach should support you in that decision.

What is the frequency of your coaching sessions? Well, that all depends upon what you and your coach decide. It is good to start with at least 6 sessions and time them every couple of weeks. Each session could be between 30-90 minutes. After that, if there are still things you are still addressing, continue at that frequency. After a while, you may find that once a month is adequate. At that point your coach is an accountability partner making sure that you are accomplishing all that you have set forth for yourself.

If you are planning to do this through work, talk to Human Resources and your Manager to see if they will pay the fees as part of your Professional Development Plan. They may also have a list of preferred trusted coaches who have worked with the organization.

Make sure that the coach does an assessment of you that is appropriate for the type of coaching they will be doing.

Costs vary depending upon the type of coach, the packages that they offer for time, frequency, and experience.

You will find fees will run between $150 – $350 per session. A session, as mentioned before will last between 30-90 minutes. 50 minutes is optimum!

Here are some resources for you to find a coach:

http://www.findacoach.com/

http://www.findyourcoach.com/index.php

http://www.coachfederation.org/

http://www.findacoachonline.com/

http://www.coachinc.com/coachu/find%20a%20coach/default.asp?s=1

And if you prefer, I have a valuable coaching partner www.questiam.com. Questiam will help you, to clarify your needs, and refer you elsewhere if you are not sure…without pressure or commitment. It is our pleasure to give you this option as a resource for your growth.

If the budget says there is no way for you to hire a coach, I strongly recommend an accountability partner of some kind. Someone you feel safe with; who will maintain confidentiality, which is wise and non judgmental. You will need this person to assist you and bounce ideas around during the course of this workbook. Start thinking about who that will be. At the end of this workbook in **Appendix A**, I have listed some guidelines for the Accountability Partner/Coach to follow in order to make your experience the best it can be. You may copy the Appendix A page and discuss it with that intended Partner/Coach.

Here is what some people have said about their coaching experiences:

Coaching is extremely beneficial to me professionally. I am now more efficient and effective in my role at work and with colleagues. The coach experience was extremely worthwhile. This is my 23rd year in my career and I can't believe that 4 x 50 minute conversations have changed how I do business to be more effective and reflective. Brian, Ontario

Based on the types of questions the coach asked me, I was able to dig deeper into myself and understand why I reacted the way I did – without her asking me these questions, I would never have been able to identify the root cause and address it in a positive way. Director, Ontario

In my personal experience with these sessions, I truly believe that the coach makes a huge difference and I was extremely happy with mine. Because of that I would categorized these session as a great learning experience.

I found personal contact and direct opinion from the coach extremely important.

My coach was fantastic in setting up a very relax environment which allow me to discuss my issues openly and for as long as I needed.

My coach was very accurate with assessments. Her recommendations and suggestions were extremely helpful.

Sr. Director, Ontario

Clean My Tools

Growth is the only evidence of life. —John Henry Newman

What Do I Do Now?

Determine what kind of coach you need. Circle one. Or circle more, depending on your need. Some of the definitions of the different types of coaches have been taken from Wikipedia.

Business Coach - Business Coaches often help businesses grow by creating and following a structured, strategic plan to achieve agreed upon goals. Multiple organizations train professionals to offer business coaching to business owners who may not be able to afford large coaching firm prices.

Leadership Coach –Leadership Coaches create the emotional energy required to gather and direct the efforts of individuals for an attainment of a goal. They teach you the difference between managing and leading in every area of your day-to-day operation. They look at your present personality, they help you understand each team member and their different needs, desires, approaches, values and belief systems to create the best productivity your team can manage.

Sales Coach – Sales Coaches will provide you with understanding and role-play to overcome objections and help you approach the client with your and their objectives in mind. The coach helps you to listen to the client's needs, identify the client's emotions about the product or service and then?

Life Coach - Life Coaching is a future-focused practice with the aim of helping clients determine and achieve personal goals. Life coaches use multiple methods that will help clients with the process of setting and reaching goals.

Emotional Intelligence Coach – Sometimes called a Transformational Coach. A Transformational Coach incorporates many modalities available in meeting the needs of the client, from business best practices to personal growth to even spiritual matters. This help may increase awareness and success in transforming one's life. People in transition often want to address deeper convictions about what they want out of life; they want more self-awareness and self-improvement. This type of coach aims to bring together and highlight all the possibilities that will help mold and shape the visioneering process for clients as they create a plan and execute the daily, weekly, monthly and yearly details.

Accountability Partner – Someone you feel comfortable with, who does not pose a threat. Someone with whom you can be authentic and with whom there is no retribution for stating how you feel about a specific person or subject. Name a couple of people here:

Career Coach - a Career Coach should be thought of as your job search partner. He/she is there to (1) help you explore and better define your professional competencies, (2) address personal issues impacting your career, (3) clearly identify your career objectives,

Financial Coach – picture Suzie Orman! This coach will be able to support and guide you through the financial world. They know where the pitfalls are, and use tried and tested strategies to help you manage your money better and make the most of it.

Nutrition and Physical Fitness Coach: in the world of health and wellness, a Health Coach is an emerging new role. Health coaching is becoming recognized as a new way to help individuals "manage" their illnesses and conditions, especially those of a chronic nature.

In both sports and health, a "coach" is a person who observes, gives objective feedback, teaches, helps to develop a plan of action and holds another responsible for their actions and commitments.

The coach will use special techniques, personal experience, expertise and encouragement to assist the coachee in bringing his/her behavioral changes about.

During the review of the second edition on this book, I have hired a Health Coach. That coach has been a great help in pointing me to new products, ideas and revealing hidden patterns that sabotage my goals. Your coach will do the same!

What are the benefits of coaching for me?

Are there cons of obtaining a coach?

What is it that I really want to work on? If I don't know, what do others (your manager, peers, significant other, children) say you should pay attention to?

What is the cost to me or my organization if I don't do this?

Deborah R. Monroe

How long will this take me to implement?

List five coaches you will contact and when you will contact them.

Have we discussed and set goals for our coaching sessions?

Has my coach given me assignments to work on in between our sessions? If not, why not?

BLADE #4

The Art Of Listening

"I know that you believe you understand what you think I said, but I'm not sure you realize that what you heard is not what I meant." — Robert McCloskey

There has been a great deal written on this subject and still, we are challenged in this area. I experience it on a daily basis from the cashier at the local grocery store to family or folks at work. I know a great deal about listening, because at one point in my life people told me that they didn't feel that I listened to them. I had no idea what they were talking about! I heard every word they said…or did I? I could sit behind my computer typing, while someone came into my office and started to speak to me. I was so talented that I could look at them in the eye, nod my head, and answer their questions, while I was still typing away without missing a key or a beat. That is how good I was, until, the comments started flying around the office that I "never listened" to anyone.

It has often been said that God gave us two ears and one mouth, because it is twice as hard to listen than it is to talk. Another definition along those same lines is that we should be listening twice as much as we should be talking. For anyone who has a relationship with a "talker", they wish that were true.

What we do know is that in the culture of North America, we mostly listen with the intent to respond. In other words, we wish you would just shut up so that we could tell you about what we have to say. It is a fatal flaw in our culture. It is aggravating and frustrating. It leads to great miscommunication, which lengthens our days, destroys our deadlines, and creates unnecessary strife.

I believe that there are several reasons why we don't listen as well as we should. You can circle or check all that apply to you.

I am too tired and my head doesn't work

I am bored with the subject matter

I can't get a word in edgewise, they talk too much

I am late for a meeting and have to go

I already know what they are going to say

I have encountered this, and I already know the solution

They have nothing I want to hear anyway

I don't believe a word they say, I don't trust them

I have too much to do and they are wasting my time

They just say the same things over and over and over

I feel threatened and I shut down so I don't have to hear what they say

All I hear is blah, blah, blah….

I know the answer and they don't so I wish they would just shut up

I am too busy formulating a response to hear the question being asked

Oh, the list goes on. Yet, go back thru this one and figure out when you are at risk of not being fully present to listen. At least that will provide a clue when you are at risk of not listening.

There are several different types of listening competencies. There are very different ways to listen, not just with our ears. There are different ways to hear what is at the heart of the matter, so let's take a look at a couple of them. We will begin with the act of listening.

The Act Of Listening

Even if you have not already read, **Stephen Covey's**, *Seven Habits of Highly Effective People*, you have probably heard a couple of these states of listening in your every day conversations. As per Mr. Covey and Deborah Monroe:

- Hearing but ignoring

- Pretending to listen: saying, "yes", "oh", "I see..." While your head is thinking about what you want for lunch.

- Selective listening: listening for key words and phrases to help resolve an issue or choosing to hear only what we want to hear.

- Attentive listening: listening for facts in the conversation like taking notes at a lecture.

- Empathetic listening: showing empathy or ready comprehension of others' emotional states; and then acknowledging that emotion in your response.

Then there is

- Deep listening: this is where we listen for facts, emotions and the underlying human need that is not being met in the other person who is speaking. We then approach the response by helping to meet that underlying human need, acknowledging the emotion and checking what we heard as far as facts are concerned.

- Whole body listening: in addition to all of the above, we now listen with our eyes and senses. We watch micro and subtle expressions of the face, body language and use the limbic part of our brain to sense what is truly going on within a situation.

It is fine and dandy to talk about the different acts of listening, yet it means nothing if we do not apply them or know which ones to apply at a specific moment.

To give you an example of different types of listening, I thought it would be fun to share this story. I was driving my car recently to a client site at a hospital. I had never been to that location before and was unsure of the exact route of turns, lights and traffic. I realized I needed to take a left turn and was in the next lane over. I put my blinker on and had plenty of space ahead of me to change lanes. The traffic though, was heavy. Folks behind me saw that I needed to get into the left lane and began to bunch up. I expected this in New York, but not in Texas. I was holding up the traffic behind me, the pressure to move into the left lane was mounting. I edged in to the left and still the car behind me refused to listen. I really needed to get over into that lane. Eventually I used a little NY driving trick to move into the lane, which slightly scared the person behind me into submission. I don't recommend that trick unless you are a professional! What did impress me is that, I was not being listened to, nor was I being heard. I was after all headed to a hospital. I could have been going there for any number of reasons; one being an emergency and still the refusing party did not listen.

There are so many ways to listen and to hear. We have mentioned several. Most important in listening is paying attention to the needs of others and that is where we are going next on our adventure.

Being Present

To listen well is to be present in a conversation. How do I describe "present"? If I said it was to be in the moment that would be only half a definition. Being present is a soulful and physical act that requires attention and energy. It is a cognitive awareness of your "state of being".

I can pass you in the hallway at work, recognize your coming as you pass me and say, "hi, how are you doing?", with no care or thought of what I just said. I may not even look at you in the eyes as I say this. I am just not conscious of the moment. I am otherwise involved in my head.

Or I can greet you with being present. I call this, "**coming up**". I come up to my eyes; I come up to my face, so that you can see *me*, not just my body. It really is not a metaphysical thing. It is just an awareness that says, "I am here".

You notice it the most when you are walking through a store shopping. You are in your own world hanging out inside of you, pondering the products on the shelves and the sodium content of soup. You see the people around you, whether you acknowledge them or not, "you" are hanging out somewhere else. Then suddenly, you see a friend, someone you have not seen in a long time. There is a change in your posture; your eyes light up, there is a smile that is sincere and genuine beaming from one side of your face to the other. "You" have *come up* into your face and are now present.

It is said that the eyes are the windows of the soul. When someone is present, it is as if Windex was just used to clear away all the dust and grime and behold, there is the person, the whole person, looking out at their friend in the store. Their eyes are alive, not dull and lifeless.

I am judged to be a happy person, on most days. You will find me smiling 75% of the time. You will find me present in that same amount. You will find my eyes, the "window to the soul", open and engaged with the rest of the world during those times. Most of my adult life I have heard these two things when I travel:

"You have the most amazing smile, it is so good to see someone smile. Why are you smiling?"

And

Do I know you? You looked at me like you know me!

Either people will be very happy when they say this to me or they will say it with cynicism, or even anger. If they respond with anger, I interpret their comment as, "why should you be so happy, what are you so freaking happy about"? It is a sad commentary that we get mad at people who are present and alive, don't you think?

To be present is to make YOU vulnerable with the intention of attaching yourself to other humans. It shows that you care and are interested. To care and to be interested shows that you want to learn about others and their points of view. It unnerves people. It also opens other people up to telling you about themselves, even if they were not expecting to do so.

I have been criticized for being this way. "Deborah, you don't have to say hello to everyone you meet"; "Deborah, you treat people like they are your friends, even if you don't know them, you are so fake." Ah, the judgments!

Just so you know it is not fake. I really do look at people as if I know them because I do want to know them, whether they are a parking attendant, a maid at a hotel or working the register at Wal-Mart. I want to be present. I want to feel connection with other human beings. I want to engage them. And yet, I also know that it takes a great deal of energy to be this way and I get tired and need my crash time to refuel.

For all of us, to be present or to have ourselves "come up" in a conversation or when listening, shows respect and honor to the other person. Do it, even if you are angry or upset with that person. Hear what they have to say in full. Go beyond selective listening into deep listening; listen for the need of the other person and where they want to be met. When you meet the need, you will find that the emotion will change and their behavior will follow. A great resource for this type of listening is **Marshal Rosenberg** creator of the concept of *Non Violent Communication*. He has taught me well, how to listen for need and not simply to look at behavior and emotion.

Mirroring Or Paraphrasing

We all have different definitions of the same things. I often do an exercise in my classes when I ask everyone to write down a number. The number they are to write down answers this question, "How many people live in a small town or what is the population of a small town"? Inevitably, I receive answers ranging from 100 people to 250,000 people. There is no right answer. There is no wrong answer, I say, there is only your answer. Out of 10 people, I will get 9 different answers. Out of 20 people, I will get 17 different answers. On a consistent basis, this little exercise shows the same results, no matter where I do it or with whom I do it.

The reason for this is that we all have different definitions of the same thing. This is based upon our own experiences, judgments, culture, paradigms, mind-sets, schema, values, or beliefs, what ever you want to call it. The challenge comes that we assume that we know what someone else means because we have defined who they are or what they have said based upon our own interpretation and understanding of the world around us. To do so is self serving and egotistical. It also lacks understanding and wisdom. Most of the time we do not do this pre-defining on purpose, we do it because we don't remember or do not have time.

I recently heard a story of a little girl who was with her grandparents. The grandmother taught the little girl how to count to ten! Proudly the little girl went to her grandfather and with great enthusiasm exclaimed, "Grandpa! I can count to ten! 1,2,3,4,5,6,7,8,9,10"!!!!

Grandpa was very impressed and looked at his adorable grandchild and with a challenge in his voice said, "Ah, yes you can! Now can you count to ten backwards?"

The little girl thought for a minute and then proceeded to count to ten and walk backwards at the same time saying, "Look Grandpa! I can count to ten backwards…."! This example is cute and yet is exactly the decoding issue that is present in so many of our conversations.

I work with managers whose complaints are that they will give an assignment to a subordinate. They will ask, "Do you understand the scope of the project?" The answer they hear is "yes." Then the direct report walks out of their office to get to work. Two weeks later, the subordinate comes back in, project complete. You look it over only to see that it is completely different than what you asked for in the beginning. You get mad, bite your tongue; you have thoughts of pouncing on the poor person in your office. Your project is late, you are now embarrassed because you have to go to your boss with a project that is incomplete and of course, you missed the deadline. We cannot put the blame on the subordinate, believe it or not. This is something that you as a manager could have thwarted had you used your mirroring or paraphrasing skills.

In the simplest of terms, this skill requires you to:

- Be present enough to ask questions

- If you are the communicator, ask others to repeat back the specifics of what they heard in their own language.

- If you are the one who is being communicated to, summarize every part of what you are hearing and then ask if you missed anything.

I know this sounds simplistic. If I had to guess, though, regarding all the people I have coached, this is one of the least known and practiced skills for communication and listening. Yet it is the one with the biggest return on investment.

Hearing vs. Listening

We have all heard, "you never listen to me". I want to propose that you do listen and you may even hear 50% of what that person is saying. The issue is when you hear, "you never listen to me", what is being said is that the other person is not *feeling heard*. That is where the problem truly lies.

We need to acknowledge that we have listened so that the other person *feels* heard. This is critical when dealing with difficult behavior in co-workers, spouses, significant others, children, customers and other types of human beings. If one does not feel heard, the chance of moving the issue forward to a resolution is slim to none. We use deep listening or empathic listening to help others feel listened to. We use our mirroring skills here. And most importantly, this must be done with genuine sincerity, or you will certainly suffer and things can progress down a deep dark path.

Simple steps are:

- Honor the other person's emotions by stating what that emotion is e.g. "I see you are frustrated by this" or "wow, you sound so excited about this"!

- Be present and ask questions around the subject that the other person is talking about.

- If you do not agree with what they are saying, a disagreement does not have to ensue. You will want to align yourself with that person by stating, "I see you feel very strongly about that and I understand why".

Listening For Life

If we are going to make the changes we desire, we need to learn how to listen and listen well. Believe it or not, if you do not know how to listen people know it and they talk about it and that means they talk about you. They will not feel respected or valued. At work, we find that if a person does not feel valued, they do not give their best performance.

When someone wants to talk to you:

- Turn away from what you are doing.

- Move away from the computer.

- Turn the phone off and sound down on your computer.

- Stand up to speak with them or sit next to them, get away from your desk.

- Give them eye contact and come up to be present.

- Decide what type of listening you will need to provide depending upon the circumstance.

- Ask them questions about what they are saying to keep you engaged.

- Summarize what you heard them say or ask them to do the same if you have communicated something of importance to them.

- Acknowledge and honor their emotion.

- Thank them for sharing or telling you what they did.

There are times when you do not have the time or the where-with-all to listen. You may be on your way to a meeting and don't have the time. In this case do not martyr yourself by standing there tapping your foot or glancing at your watch. A simple response will suffice. You can put this one in the playbook and use it anytime you need:

> *"I am on my way to a meeting. I really want to hear what you have to say, so let's make some time later this afternoon when I can give you my full attention."*

This statement tells the truth. It also tells the other person that they are important enough to warrant your full attention and that you want to hear what they have to say. They will leave you feeling appreciated and valued instead of frustrated because you are too rushed to hear what they have to say. And, that is a winning place to be with anyone.

Clean My Tools

"Everything has been said before, but since nobody listens we have to keep going back and beginning all over again."—Andre Gide

In this section our concentration was on different aspects of listening. We want to go a little deeper and find out when you are at risk of not listening, or being present. One of your tasks this month is to keep tabs on this by using the form below. You can recreate it with a spreadsheet if you like, to have it at hand throughout the month.

1. Complete this exercise. Use memorable moments during the next two weeks.:

Was I listening?	Which type of listening did I use?	Who was it with?	What was I thinking?	What was I feeling?
No	Selective	Ronnie	Oh, come on, you already told me this	Aggravated and annoyed

It is important for us to find out to whom and when you are not listening. You will want to speak to your coach or accountability partner about specific strategies to overcome your responses to these situations. During maintenance at the end of the month, take some time to write down the key themes and people who cause the reaction in you not to listen.

Go to at least three people who know you well and ask them, "*do you consider me to be a good listener and why?*" (manager, peer, direct report, family member, key client).

Write down what you hear them say and consider the changes you may need to make. Do not become defensive if you hear something that you don't like. Just let people talk and take notes like you are doing some market research. This is not the time to stand up and be defensive. Let them talk.

Practice Being Present

What do you need to do in order to ensure that you are fully present and paying attention in each of your conversations? Do you need an accountability partner to keep you on track? If yes, who will that be?

How do you need to tweak your behavior and attitude to be much more aware and attentive?

Mirroring/ Paraphrasing

Start with your manager. The next time you have a conversation around a project use this skill for yourself. Make sure to have at least two conversations with your manager in the first two weeks of working on this section. Begin to practice doing this with other people, like direct reports and children the last half of the month.

What will happen if I do not invest the time to change this habit?

Wouldn't it be nice to finally hear someone say to you, you are a great listener! If you have not heard that in a while…let's hope that by the end of this month, you have created enough of a change to see the difference. Remind yourself that it is the small, consistent, incremental changes that cause the big re-formations to bloom and grow.

Maintenance

"Listen or thy tongue will keep thee deaf" — Indian Proverb

Review your spreadsheet. Write down the key themes of when you didn't listen and to whom you did not listen well.

What did you discover?

What changes do you think you can make to change your reaction to these situations or people? (If you are struggling with this question, bounce it around with a coach or accountability partner).

When you interviewed others about your listening skills, what was the greatest impacting piece of information you heard. What did you start to change based on that feedback. How did the feedback make you feel?

Did you use mirroring with your manager: Did it go well? Were you present in the conversation? Did you actively ask questions and use attentive or active listening?

With others: what was it like asking them to clarify for you? Did you notice a difference for them in their understanding? Were there any disconnects that could have gone awry, yet were saved by mirroring?

Deborah R. Monroe

What changes have you noticed in your own listening behavior?

What benefits have you experienced by listening more adeptly? Has anyone commented as yet on the changes you have made in this area?

BLADE #5

What Is Coming Out Of My Mouth?

"People may not remember what you say, yet they will always remember how you made them feel!" -**The name of the wise originator of this quote cannot be found so it remains anonymous until then!**

"Loose lips sink ships"; "out of the heart the mouth speaks"; "actions speak louder than words", are just a few familiar parts of speech that we have heard on a daily basis since we were children. I am a true believer that our words have power to create or tear apart. The old adage, *"sticks and stones may break my bones, but words will never hurt me"*, is one of the biggest lies to befall mankind. This section addresses the affect and effect our words have on others and on ourselves.

The physicist **David Boehm** said this and it stopped me in my tracks when I read this statement from his work the ***Implicate Order***,

"Our language and our nervous system combine to constantly construct our environment. Language is like another set of eyes and hands for the nervous system, through which we coordinate actions with others. We exist in language. It is by languaging and recurrent action or human practices that we create meaning together."

Those are powerful words and a poignant message. In this section we will explore some of the important contributions you can make to yourself and others concerning what comes out of your mouth!

Say What You Mean And Do What You Say

You would think that this topic would be a no brainer and for many of us it is. However, I believe it must be addressed. Increasingly, I see and hear people lying to me, telling me one thing and then doing another. It aggravates the heck out of me, if you really want to know! "I will send you the contract by next week..." next week comes and the contract doesn't arrive. I then need to follow up and follow up until I feel like a nag. So the simple lesson here is if you are going to say you are going to do something, do it, even if it is inconvenient. Your word is your bond.

Now understand, I know that things come up, I know there are emergencies, I know that we must to remain flexible in this day and time and of course, there are also considerations for mistakes. Unfortunately, for the most part, we do not honor this code. We must stop this. If we don't have our word, what do we have?

I was at a holiday party many years ago. Some of my peers and friends had gathered from all over the country for this Wednesday night bash. We hardly get to see one another so the joy of our reunion was full of, "oh, you look great", and "how long has it been?" Greetings with huge smiles and enthusiastic voices, bright eyes and Cosmopolitans (fancy drink) in hand were all on the menu. And boy, did those Cosmopolitans taste like Kool-Aid! Very, very rarely do I drink enough to be sorry, yet here we were in New York City, friends gathered, the chill in the Holiday air and I let things get away from me with the drinking. After we all left the party we decided to go down to Grand Central Station to one of the little clubs there for a nightcap. I persuaded my good friend Keplyn to stay for one more *salute!* "Ah, Deb" she said with sorrow, "I have to get up in the morning and teach a class. I can't stay for one more". With enthusiasm that only comes with an overt amount of *Cosmos*, my reply was "Come on Kep! If you stay for one more, I will teach the first chapter of the course for you in the morning!" Really? Are you nuts? Yes, that is what I agreed to. I did not however, realize the lateness of the evening or the effects of the evening's folly that would begin to manifest itself fully as I entered my hotel room for the night. I do confess the room was spinning around. I used that little trick of putting one's foot on the floor to steady my equilibrium...to no avail! When the alarm went off hours later I woke up in a similar state, which included a massive headache and nauseous stomach. Please don't judge me; I am sharing this for our growth!

After a piece of dry toast and tea, I made it to Keplyn's classroom feeling like I was run over by a concrete truck. As I took the class over to begin the first chapter, Keplyn looked at me with wonder and amazement, "I can't believe you are here…I really didn't think you would make it!" Yet, I said that I would be there and even if it hurt me and it did, I wanted to fulfill my words to my friend.

Understand that I share this with you not to boast. There have been many times I have not done what I said I would. The example here is a simple lesson about, *"watch what you say when you are drinking"*! No…not really! It is a lesson that our character comes in all sizes and to show it we sometimes must "swear to our own hurt" or keep our promises even when it hurts us to do so.

Before you tell someone you are going to do something, give yourself *space* to consider, "Can I make this commitment, with these resources, within this timeframe", etc. If you are unable to do it, make sure you are honest and forthright and tell the other person why you have your doubts about it. Explaining why you cannot is much more effective than simply stating that you can't.

Use Your Words

Some of the executives I work with don't talk when they are upset. They "growl". They make actual growling noises to say they are upset, frustrated or "have had it". The first approach we can take is to find what that growl represents as an emotion. The growl may indeed be just that, or the grow could manifest itself a rolling of the eyes or a flared nostril, or even a deep breath passing reluctantly through a tightened jaw and clenched teeth.

A growl is what it is. It says to those around you, "beware, I am about to bite someone". When people recognize these things about you, it can be what triggers them and makes them either not want to listen to you or to run away as fast as they possibly can in the opposite direction.

To be authentic, we want to turn these noises or physical "tells" into words. If you are frustrated, say you are frustrated. If you need some time to think about something and how you feel about that, then say so. Grow the growl into actual words that express what is truly going on. You will find the people around you will react with greater acceptance to words than with ancient hostile noises coming from your mouth and threatening glances!

And remove the word "try" from your vocabulary! The word *try* means nothing. It is the most uncommitted word in the English language in my opinion. The word *try* actually has the power to change your body chemistry. I will save that exercise for another time, yet from the words of one of my most favorite movie aliens, **Yoda** (from the movie Star Wars), ***"Do or do not, there is no try"***. In other words, let your "yes be yes" and your "no be no". Let's stop the wishy-washy uncommitted speech that means nothing and scoop up our honor and character by doing what we say and saying what we mean.

Sarcasm

As fatal flaws go, this one is one of the top three. If you have a tendency to use sarcasm please note this section with a bright green highlighter.

Let's look at what sarcasm really is. Definition:

Sarcasm –noun

1. Harsh or bitter derision or irony.

2. A sharply ironical taunt; sneering or cutting remark: a review full of sarcasms.

If we go deeper into the meaning of the word, the Latin root of sarcasm is *sarco*, which means *tearing of the flesh*.

Looking further into this we find that sarcasm stemmed from *sarcasmos* or *sarkazein*, which means ripping or tearing away of the flesh. Both *sarcasmos* and *sarkazein* was a form of torture used in ancient medieval times.

I wonder if the last part of the word, chasm is rooted in *chasm*, a deep divide or gulf, a marked separation or division. It seems that can be the result of using sarcasm in our relationships.

Yes, I have coached many people that thrive on sarcasm. They think it is funny. They say it relieves stress in the room and makes people laugh. What they don't see is that people are laughing because they are too uncomfortable not to. They do not want to upset the status quo. In addition, I have watched careers destroyed or at the least, stifled by those who use this particular tool. It is best to avoid it all together.

This is not a tool that will bring life, value and productivity to the office or other relationships, is it? Why do we use sarcasm? We have pondered this question for millennium, I am sure. What the experts have said is that we use it to cloak our own insignificance or insecurities. Who knows why this has been an accepted part of corporate culture. What I can say to encourage you is to inhibit its use and find something else to laugh about.

As a teenager, growing up in England, I often heard it said that *sarcasm is the lowest form of wit.* I really didn't understand that until I was the brunt of the sarcasm. If indeed one is working on making a cohesive dynamic team, sarcasm is the last thing needed in the mix. The emotions used in sarcasm are contempt and disdain, again, not productive or pretty to those around us. As a leader, the results we are seeking in others are their ability to trust us, trust what we say and know that we are there to protect them. These are some of the responsibilities of a leader that can be undone in an instant with sarcasm. If you are one who suffers under someone who uses sarcasm, take them aside gently and say this:

> *"I know it is not your intention to hurt anyone with sarcasm, yet I can see that the impact that it has on the team is not getting the intended results. We can think of another way to break the stress in our meetings together".*

If you are the one dishing out the sarcasm, I hope this section has inspired you to cut back and consider the objectives you have in creating that team dynamic, whether at work, with friends or at home. As you begin to inhibit the sarcastic responses, it is going to get tough. You will think of all the great comebacks, the great lines you want to push out of your mouth. You may be successful in holding them back only 20% of the time. If you can do that, you are well on your way to a major switch. Be proud of yourself. We have a great exercise for you in **Clean My Tools**. Once you begin to appropriate this you will be astonished at how people begin to react to you.

Remember, you are a leader (we all are in our own ways) and what you do spreads like a virus, so after you deal with this yourself, you may have to go and clean up the mess that was created by the sarcasm and re-teach the people around you how not to use it.

Even If It Makes Your Hair Curl, Be Honest With Others.

In section one, we spent some time talking about being honest with yourself. Now we will turn our attention to being honest with others. The lesson here is to be honest in a way that is palatable for the other person and gets the results that are best for everyone.

Being honest is not about being nice. It is not about being nasty either. There are times when we can create an atmosphere of codependence and dysfunction within our organization when we are afraid to be honest.

The key to being honest with others is saying your truth and not blaming the other person. It does not require that you begin your sentence with the word "honestly…" or "can I be honest with you?" If you are having difficulty with someone's behavior or an attitude, approach it from your point of view. Say, "When I encounter this behavior, it makes me feel uncomfortable". Note that the word **you** is not mentioned in that sentence.

Honesty reveals the hidden miscommunications and needs that we have with one another. Things that stay in the dark grow and spread and then manifest into nasty boogiemen! We are unable to succeed in the way we want to because of it.

One organization I have worked with had a problem with being "too" nice. People don't get what they need because they are afraid they are going to hurt someone's feelings. The managers are not masterful at saying what they mean. It is sugarcoated communication that keeps others from really approaching their peak performance.

Other scenarios that I have experienced happen when those who tell their truth do so with blame and fear. They are honest to a fault, but not with their own feelings. They blame the dysfunction or miscommunication on someone else, never themselves. It is possible to tell the truth with grace, expressing the impact that the other's behavior has on you. Your coach can help you practice this to get the language of "telling the truth with grace" down to an art.

No one deserves to be lied to. Say what you mean, say it from your perspective and don't blame the other person for the way that you feel.

A wonderful friend of mine, **Blair Steinbach**, says it this way,

"No one does things TO you. They do things FOR themselves"

When we are honest with grace much of the miscommunication and feelings we are holding in will clear and we can get back to work on the things that matter.

Valiant Exchanges

There comes a time in all of our lives when we have to have one of "those conversations"! Great books have been written and fabulous courses have helped us to choose the words we want to use when we have a valiant exchange. Some call it a *Courageous Conversation*; others call it *The Art of Conversatin' (say this one with a Southern US accent)!* Whatever it is called this is a conversation that you may need to have when you are the one at risk of loosing something. I call it a *Valiant Exchange*. Why? Because it takes guts to have this type of conversation; it takes a warrior's heart and courage; it takes a fearless approach, as this type of conversation may not go as you intend.

The conversation could go well if the words, tone, and intention are well formed. Otherwise, this type of conversation has the potential to change your world, and not in a good way. If it does go that way, you will need to stand by your convictions, believe that what you said was your truth and be happy with that. There is no telling how the other party will react or even more importantly, what they will hear through their own filters or "decoder".

I have tried having this conversation in many different ways and forms. Sometimes the outcome has been as intended and other times the conversation has led me to walk down paths unknown. Ultimately this has brought me to the place I stand now. Whether the outcome has been what I expected or not, there was always freedom and life in them. In the end, I was honest and said how I felt; said how I saw the situation, and one can not ask more of a human being than to have courage when faced with risk to speak one's truth.

I struggle with this topic. It goes back to when I was a child. Children were to be seen not heard, if you didn't have anything nice to say, you didn't say it, what ever platitude you want to use, it always seemed to me that when I opened my mouth I got into trouble. So I learned not to say how I truly felt, beyond that, I really didn't have the emotional vocabulary that I have now, so I probably would have made a mess of it anyway.

As an adult, I have learned to begin these types of exchanges by stating my intentions and asking them to listen. Once that is out in the air and understood, I begin the conversation with how "I" feel about the issue and if I am afraid to talk about it, I will say, I am afraid to talk about it. I tell them what I am struggling with. Then whether artfully or clumsily I will state what I would like to see as a resolution.

Thereafter, if the other person has not freaked out or run out of the room, I ask them a question about how they think we can approach the subject to resolve the issue at hand. There are four steps listed below that can create an artful way to discuss difficult topics and use a team approach to finding a resolution.

Don't be deceived. There will always be emotion that arises when Valiant Exchanges occur. The mature reaction is that the person sits and listens. These steps require deep and whole body listening. This requires listening for the need of the other and understanding how to cross the bridge of discontent and hurt without bungee jumping over the edge without a bungee cord.

However it goes and whatever the outcome, the most important thing is that you are true to yourself. You refuse to be a victim of circumstance thus, remaining shutdown by fear. That is to be applauded my friend. That is to be applauded!

Before you ever have a Valiant Exchange, please let me suggest a couple of things that you can do for yourself in preparation:

- Determine your intention. Why are you having this conversation?

- Write down what your intention is.

- Write down how you are feeling about the whole thing. Be authentic.

- Write down the result you want to achieve from the conversation.

- Schedule the time to have the conversation during the time of the day when you are at your best; awake, alert and aware.

- Before you have the conversation, eat something, take a short walk and drink at least eight ounces of water. The brain needs the sugar, the electrical system in the brain needs the water and the little walk will provide more oxygen to the brain for crisper, clearer thinking and responding.

- Go for it!

If during the conversation, things are not going well. It is ok to pull the plug and start over or to call it off and do it again another day when emotions have settled. If you pull the plug, use verbiage that creates consideration and empathy. Don't get up and leave in a huff while mumbling under your breath. That will just make a difficult thing worse, don't you think?

When we master the art of the Valiant Exchange, in essence we master ourselves and show the world that we are indeed not cowards or victims, but are valuable, important and worth taking the risk. This does not always manifest itself the first time you try. As, with anything, the more practice that goes into it, the greater the result and comfort.

I suggest you begin practicing the steps above in conversations involving less complex issues that are not emotionally charged and carry less risk. This will simply help you get comfortable with the concepts and delivery in order to build the skills and turn the Valiant Exchange into an art.

The Right-Wrong Trap

There are many times in business when we come to the conclusion that our solution is right and the other person's solution is wrong. This happens even more so in personal relationships with that special someone. "Why do you always have to be right?"…as said with anger and frustration from the other party. Your response, "Because I always am".

Even if you are always right, there is something to be said about being humble and even considerate of the other person. Even more so, is the challenge that if you are indeed "right", then someone is always going to be "wrong". And that is a trap. Can two people be "right" at the same time? Absolutely. Can two people be "wrong" at the same time? Affirmative!

The mess created here is that we get stuck with being right and the other person wrong and we never look up to see how we are going to meet our objective.

Petra was a client of mine on the west coast. At that time my company was offering software training. The focus of the work consisted of helping the client with a software upgrade rollout. We were to train their entire staff on all the changes in the software. It was an intensive schedule and I had three or four trainers present for a couple of weeks with multiple classes scheduled per day.

Petra was a difficult customer from my subjective point of view. She exhibited control as a type of nitpicker. I am being nice when I say that! Training, adult education, professional development, etc. is my business. It has been my business in one form or another for longer than I want to admit. I understand the process of training and delivery to adults, instructional design and all the things that go into my chosen profession. Petra didn't think I did and that was fine…or at least that is what I told myself. She would berate my trainers, who were the top-shelf type of trainers. She would berate me and if I said something back in response, her reply was, "I don't' feel comfortable with this conversation" and then hang up on me. Sometimes I had to ask myself, "Why am I doing this?" because there is no amount of money that was going to make that situation okay!

During one of the conversations with Petra it got really intense. I realized that I was in that "right-wrong" trap with her and because of her total desire to have to be right. I was at a loss as to how to change the situation to meet the objective, which was to have a successful training rollout. I moved myself away from having to be right in this situation. I suggested to Petra that we look at how to meet her objectives. Her stated objective was that she wanted everything to be perfect. From that point, I could ask her questions about what that looked like to her and what her expectations were of the trainers. I was able to focus on helping us both make decisions based upon the outcomes that were desired, rather than making decisions based upon the situation at hand, including who needed to be right or wrong.

The end result of this change was that we protected her status and expectations and saved her embarrassment by being the proven professionals that we are. In the process of doing so, we found out why Petra reacted so intensely to the whole training project.

Evidently, she had hired someone else the year before and that experience turned out to be a nightmare. Petra took a hit on her reputation in the company and was put on a tight leash with her choices and performance. Her emotional motivator was fear that turned into the behavior of control. All that was made manifest to meet her underlying need of shelter, food and water…life's sustenance. To lose her job because of our performance was no option and she was going to make darn sure that did not happen. We then became the focus of her need and the ones with power to take her job away. That is why we endured her behavior. If I had only known that up front, I could have managed my own reactions with greater ease, given her greater empathy and taken a different approach instead of allowing her to drive us all nuts.

I see that success is all in what we focus on. We can look at a situation and argue, "I'm right." "No I'm right." Or we can say, "Where do we need to go and how are we going to get there", regardless of whom is feeling obligated to be correct. In other words, do you want to get it done or do you want to be right?

So many projects, lives and relationships are thwarted by this pattern. It is my hope that we can all move past the "I'm right and you're wrong" thought processes and into the solution we desire.

Clean My Tools

> *"It is our choices that show what we truly are, far more than our abilities."* — Joanne Kathleen Rowling

This month, the concentration is around you, once again. It is so important to become self aware about all the topics in this section. As previously mentioned, when your self-awareness increases, change will come when you apply small incremental consistent changes. So let us begin!

Did I find myself acting differently at work than at home? How?

_____

_____

_____

To create an authentic you at work, what small step can you take to change that? Have you noticed your own physical tells or "growls"? What emotions do each attribute actually represent? Make a point this month to turn those into words and communicate what is really going on with you in those moments.

_____

_____

_____

Am I overwhelmed with how much I have on my plate? Is there a way that I can say no or consider my options so I don't over promise?

Who is afraid to tell me the truth? Ask those people what their experiences have been regarding me and my sarcastic remarks. Ask them what they have seen, what they have heard.

If I need to apologize to anyone, do it. Write down their names.

If I need to talk to someone about their sarcasm, who is it? When am I going to talk to them and how am I going to word my conversation?

Do I have any Valiant Exchanges that need to happen? Who is it with? Sit down and write what you are going to say to them. What are your intentions and what are your objectives?

What can I do to practice the steps before the "conversation"?

Write down a recent experience when you got stuck in the "right-wrong" trap. Looking at it now, what could you have done to change the conversation and the outcome?

Think about that person you got stuck in the "right-wrong" trap with and find out what the underlying need was that was unmet, like my example of Bonnie.

Last challenge of this section is to purchase this book and read it. It is an easy read, yet powerful beyond belief. *The Nibble Theory And The Kernel Of Power* by **Kaleel Jamison.** Happy reading! See you in 25 days or so…

Deborah R. Monroe

Maintenance

> *"The leader for today and the future will be focused on how to be – how to develop quality, character, mind-set, values, principles and courage"* — Frances Hesselbein

What did you notice this month about how your communication changed? Are you more gracious, less harsh? Are you watching the words that come out of your mouth? If so, what changed and how do you know?

Did you practice having Valiant Exchanges? What was the outcome? Are you feeling more confident in how you have one of these conversations? Where you able to tell your truth without stepping on the other person?

After you read the nibble theory what were the three biggest take aways for you? Did you see yourself in the stories she was telling? Were you the one biting or being eaten? What do you plan to do now with that knowledge? How will you change your approach?

Have you begun to give yourself space before you commit to a project, task or deed to ensure that you are able to fulfill your word? What have you done differently? What weaknesses do you need to continue to be aware of in your own responses?

BLADE #6

Build My Relationships

"Share your success and help others succeed. Give everyone a piece of the pie. If the pie's not big enough, make a bigger pie."
— *Dave Thomas, founder of Wendy's*

Perhaps you feel like you have good working relationships both inside and out of work. If you do, that is commendable! Perhaps in this section you will find a couple of tasty little additions to help you continue improving those relationships.

If you happen to need a little improvement in this area and do not know where to begin, then this section will encourage you in several ways.

Some people are almost supernatural in their ability to find the sweet spots that make each individual on their team or in their life feel valued, important, respected and invaluable. Their teams thrive, their productivity soars, they don't spend their time frustrated and wondering how to get people to do what needs to be done. They are recognized for their achievements, they are praised and we sit back wondering what they do differently to make them so "special". I have coached many of those who struggle with leading others.

It is largely possible that many of us were promoted into the jobs we have now because we are good at what we do, task-wise. We are technologically savvy; we know the business and get results. We moved into management and then had to make the teamwork and that is where we were greatly surprised. Just because we knew what we were doing, doesn't mean we knew how to manage our greatest assets, people.

Perhaps you are fine at work and the challenge for you is the teenage boy or girl at home who refuses to do anything you ask them to! Whatever the case, this section will provide some easy adjustments that will improve the situations you are facing in this area. It's all about building relationships and it is in those relationships that you find the cooperation and trust that will build the future.

Take Your Lunch

This does sound trite. Yet, it has great power in several areas. Taking lunch not only gives your brain a much needed respite and your body a rest so that you come back reenergized with creative ideas, but it also gives you time to build relationships.

Never eat lunch alone! This is a wonderful opportunity for you to get to know your staff and peers. Take Steve and Adam's stories as an example.

Steve had been a good manager for 15 years. He got results, he drove his team, he enjoyed his work, but something was missing. When I received Steve's 360 emotional intelligence assessment I could see by the results that he had low personal drive and that his self regard scored low. I prefer not to judge when I see results like this, because I want to hear what is behind the measurements. I wanted to hear his story. Steve was shy. Not only was he shy but he also was taught by his parents never to share anything about himself. So Steve was not inclined to tell anyone much about what he did or what his experiences were. The results were that neither his staff nor his manager knew much about him, except for what he did at work. That would have seemed fine 20 years ago, but in today's culture, people want to know who they are working with. The resistance to share was also viewed by others in his office as a sense of superiority and pride. The tongues were wagging in the office. It was thought that Steve was too "good" to talk about himself or care what others thought about him. As a result, things were going south for his team and their performance as a whole.

As Steve shared this with me, there was sadness in his voice. I could feel the hopelessness fill in the gaps of silence on the phone as he described how uncomfortable it was for him to share even the smallest of interesting things that he had done or accomplished in his life. I asked Steve what he thought he could share about himself, only one small thing. His silence on the phone was full of hard pressed thought and deepening fear that he would never be able to come up with anything of interest about himself. At last, he found something comfortable to share.

The next thing we had to conquer was to find a place for him to be able to share this story of himself conducive to the working environment. Steve never went to lunch. He had meetings planned, he worked at his desk while munching on a sandwich, even if he had the opportunity to go to the cafeteria, he did not. I suggested taking each of his team members out to lunch, one person per week. He was to talk to them individually before hand to set expectations that when he did ask them, it was not as a reproof and that no one was going to the "principle's office". That was as important as having him share something about himself. By doing that he was managing their expectations, thus curbing the possibility of their minds running wild with unproductive thoughts. "Steve, when you open up, they will begin to feel safe and do the same thing", I said. That is where we would start.

Steve made a point to let everyone know he wanted to have lunch with them and why. He made his appointments and once a week he spent time with one of his direct reports. To his great surprise many of the misunderstandings, judgments and mind-sets that had been held over him were squelched as his people heard him open up. He was authentic in starting this conversation with each one. He said, "I want you to know, that I know how people view me. The real reason I don't share things with people is that I am very shy about it and my coach suggested that I challenge myself by taking each one of you to lunch." Steve eased into his conversations with caution. His comfort level was more likely a five out of ten when he began and within one month that comfort level was up to an eight. The relationships he was building were based upon his being real and opening his mouth. This was no easy thing for Steve and yet within the month, he began to see the changes in those that surrounded him. People were much more communicative and warm. They were approachable and trusting. Their productivity began to improve and within a short period of time, Steve's team was one of the shining examples within his department. All that transpired, because he took the time to share himself and take his people out to lunch.

This is a small thing, yet it makes a huge impact. The same concept holds weight with family. We end up being the taskmasters at home, telling people what and what not to do and rarely, do we take the time to build the relationships with those we hold dearest.

Deborah R. Monroe

Adam was head of an IT department. When he and I began our coaching together he said he really didn't have anything to talk about or any worries at all. It soon became plain that he had a teenage son who did not want to take showers and all day long sat around playing video games. Adam would have to force his son to shower once a week, a big argument would ensue, feelings would be hurt and attitude would race around the house like a bicycle team at the Tour-de-France. I probed Adam with questions about the interactions at home. I asked him when the last time he and his son had just gone out to have fun or had a bite to eat together and when the last time was that Adam had shared anything with his son about his experience growing up; a funny story, a poignant story about his relationship with his own father. The answer was not surprising to me. It had been months since he and his son had gone out and as far as sharing; he had never done that, ever!

Adam's assignment then became, just that, take is son out for food, fun and sharing. No talking about his disheveled look or personal hygiene; just father and son hanging out for a day. Adam was petrified, although he never would have admitted it. I could feel it through the phone line.

Two weeks later, Adam called me with the first excitement I had ever heard in his voice. How did it go, I asked. He was so surprised that one little father and son moment would make such a difference. His son was now sharing information freely without Adam having to pull it out like a dentist. He was showering on his own accord and actually started doing his chores around the house. He talked to his dad about his day instead of answering the parental question of "how was your day" with the teenage response of "fine". The whole scenario improved upon every coaching call until the last when Adam said to me with great seriousness and warmth, "Deborah, this has made me a better man and a better father and for that I can never thank you enough". He didn't know it, but when I hung up the phone, my heart was pierced and there were tears in my eyes. That, I thought, is why I do what I do. I would never be the same and neither would he or his son.

Sharing a meal and a story builds relationships. You have 7 times a week to take advantage of that truth. Start thinking about which relationship you want to improve and what you are going to eat!

Learn More About The People Around You

A key intrinsic motivational factor with human beings is "knowing them". If you want to know how to motivate those around you, it is important to know who they are. There are several things you can find out by simply asking. What is their:

- Communication frequency

- Personality style

- Communication preference

- Extrinsic motivation preferences

- Intrinsic motivational appetites

Importantly, you also want to know these things about yourself as well.

Communication Frequency:

The whole concept here is simply this, how often do people need or want to communicate. You will find that some like to be in touch with you on a minute-by-minute basis. Others you may not hear from for a week or two. The important factor here is for you to know **your** frequency first. Once that is discovered, then ask the individuals in your team what they prefer.

If there is a large gap in frequencies between you and a team member you will find this information helpful to change dynamics. For example, if you are a low frequency communicator who doesn't need to be in the middle of every project and you have a low frequency person working on a project with you, there is a large chance that there could be miscommunication and mistakes made in the project, because neither party is talking.

If you are a low frequency communicator and you are working with a high frequency communicator, you may view them as "high maintenance" or very needy. They are always knocking on your door, calling you about the smallest problem and emailing you incessantly on every subject. Come to some type of agreement about when it is ok to contact you and refer them to other people who can answer their questions to manage your time with greater efficiency.

Another thing that you can teach the high frequency communicators is to come to you with solutions to their problems and not the problems themselves. One of the primary reasons that we see high frequency is fear; fear of making a mistake or not clearly understanding the task or approach to the task in front of them. You can also practice your mirroring/paraphrasing skills here as well. Take away the fear, clarify understanding, ask them questions and have them come to you with solutions. Coach them to success in this way and you will free up a great deal of your time.

The high frequency manager and low frequency employee relationship can run amuck resulting in the employee feeling micro-managed. The manager is always on top of the employee, asking why, when and how. A consensus can be reached and the manager's emotionally motivated fear of being late with a project or being seen as a failure due to the "incompetence" of an employee has to be managed.

On the other hand, the low frequency employee may need to be coached in their communication habits. Structure and boundaries will need to be set to satisfy the high frequency manager. Balance on both ends is the key to success.

The high frequency manager and high frequency employee may simply spend too much time talking and not enough time doing. We may find this with a new manager who has a new team and they are feeling their way through the vastness of new situations to avoid failure.

Personality Styles

Often I hear people say, "Deborah, I think I have some people in the wrong jobs. How do I move them around and engage them?" There are so many answers to that, yet I like to begin with personality styles.

So much information is out there surrounding this topic, some of it easy, some complicated, the most important concept about personality styles that gets lost in translation, is once you know yourself you can help meet your own needs. Once you know others, you can help meet their needs by approaching them in a way that makes sense for their specific style.

I have done a Myers Briggs analysis. I am not saying anything negative about the science. What I am going to say is that it is so complicated with 16 different styles of personality that no one person can grasp how to interact with another or even figure out who the other person is. We have DISC™, and True Colors to name a few. We have temperament assessment tools, we have career assessment tools, there are so many to choose from it makes it hard to know what to use without scorching our budgets.

I lean towards the four animal model developed by Gary Smalley and Dr. John Trent because of its humor and simplicity. Over years of use the definitions have evolved. My thanks go to Sally Wright, an old colleague, and her permission to use her initial assessment of each personality style.

Knowing that we embody all the different styles in any four-zoned assessment, only one or two of those styles float to the top as our major drivers. Here is a brief description of each of the animals:

Lions: Are Dominant And Task Oriented

The emphasis of Lions is to shape their environment by overcoming opposition to accomplish results. Typical drivers: CEO's, VP's, Directors, and Project Managers

Lions are:

- Controlling and direct

- They work at a fast pace

- Their priority is the task at hand

- They focus on results

- They become irritated when others seem to waste time

- For security they rely on being in control

- For acceptance they depend on leadership skills and strive to be winners

Lions are independent, strong willed, have high ego-strength, they prefer maximum freedom to manage self and others, have a low tolerance for feelings, attitudes and advice of others. They want immediate results, and are decisive, goal oriented, cool and competitive, accept challenges, solve problems, dislikes inaction, causes action, dominant, fast and impatient.

Lions under stress, however, can take complete control; they may tend to disregard the feelings and responsibilities of others to "get the job done". To increase their flexibility Lions need to:

- Practice good listening skills.

- Develop a slower pace and more relaxed image.

- Develop patience, humility and sensitivity.

- Focus on the needs of others.

- Explain reasons for their conclusions.

- Identify with a group.

- Be aware of existing sanctions.

Otters: Are Motivators

The emphasis of Otters is to have fun and influence others. They shape their environments by forming others into an alliance to accomplish results. They are great motivators. Typical Otters: most sales people, teachers, speakers, visionaries

Otters are:

- Supporting and direct
- Work at a fast pace
- Their priority is relationships
- Their focus is interaction and the dynamics of relationship
- Their main irritation is boring tasks and being alone
- For security they rely on flexibility
- For acceptance they depend upon playfulness

They are spontaneous in actions and decisions, stimulating, talkative, work at quick pace, gregarious, risk takers, enthusiastic, optimistic, emotional and friendly.

Otters under stress, however, will attack if they feel threatened. Their need to be accepted becomes a weakness if they cross the border of integrity. To increase their flexibility otter's need to:

- Control time and emotions.
- Develop an objective mindset.
- Give more time to checking, verifying, specifying.
- Commit to following through.
- Concentrate on the task.
- Take a more logical approach.

Golden Retrievers: Are Loyal And Supportive

Golden Retrievers rely on steadiness and cooperating with others to carry out a task. Typical Golden Retrievers: any job that entails caring for others thru relationship.

Golden Retrievers are:

- Supporting and indirect
- Work at a slow, easy and relaxed pace
- Focused on relationships as a priority
- Easily irritated by pushy, aggressive behavior
- Reassuring, guaranteeing performance
- Dependent upon close relationships
- Dependent upon conformity, loyalty and helpful in nature

Golden Retrievers accept change slowly and reluctantly, like close relationships, support and "actively" listen to others, are warm and accepting, work slowly and cohesively with others, they are agreeable, steady and calm, supportive, emphatic listeners, they share personal feelings and emotions, they approach risk cautiously, they have good counseling skills, are slow to take action and make decisions, dislike interpersonal conflict, have excellent ability to gain support from others, they are patient and considerate, loyal and dependable, warm and friendly, they prefer first names and informality, they ask many questions are amiable, consistent and respectful.

Golden Retrievers under stress, however, may take the "doormat" approach. Their loyalty may cause them to not say "no" at appropriate times. They may be unable to make decisions or confront individuals. To increase their flexibility Golden Retrievers need to:

- Say no occasionally.
- Be willing to move out of their comfort zone into conflict.
- Complete tasks without over sensitivity to others' feelings.
- Take risks.
- Delegate to others.

Beavers: Are Detailed and Self Contained

Beavers work with existing circumstances to promote quality in products or service. Typical Beavers: research scientists, accountants, compliance officers and the like.

Beavers are:

- Controlling and indirect
- Slow, steady, methodical workers
- Task oriented
- Irritated by surprises and unpredictability
- Reliant on preparation
- Dependent upon being correct

Beavers are serious, persistent, orderly, perfectionist, they seek facts and data and have a "show me" attitude, they are structured and organized, they ask specific questions about specific details, they want to be right, therefore rely heavily on data collection, have good problem-solving skills, they concentrate on detail, are diplomatic with others and critical of performance, they comply with authority, are cautious in action and decision making, they like organization and structure, they dislike too much involvement, they work at a slow cautious pace are time disciplined and precise, they prefer objective, task-oriented, intellectual work environments, they like to work alone slowly and precisely, they follow directions and standards and check constantly for accuracy.

Beavers under stress, however, can become paralyzed with fear of making a mistake; they may override the feelings of others in their desire to do a perfect job. To increase their flexibility Beavers need to:

- Openly show appreciation and concern for others.
- Try some shortcuts and timesavers.
- Adjust the work done on a project to align with the outcomes.

- Learn to adjust to change and disorganization.
- Work on decision making skills and initiating new possibilities.
- Negotiate rather than take a hard line.

When I am speaking or facilitating a course, I tend to take on a mix of Lion and Otter. I need to manage a group dynamic and I want to motivate the learning process. At home I am more of a Golden Retriever personality, laid back, hospitable and enjoy more flexibility. The Beaver personality for me is a learned coping mechanism for business. I still struggle with the details, as I am more of a conceptual thinker than a linear thinker.

I have the right personality for my chosen profession. I had it confirmed doing a "Strong's Inventory" of my skill set and personality based upon being similar to others in my field. God forbid you ask me to sit down and write the detailed set of instructions for Standard Operating Procedures, I could do it and it might take me forever, but it would not be a joy. I would get bored quickly and want to leave that project to invite people to a party!

Put people in the jobs that match their personality, learning styles and energy. If you have a lot of Beavers on your team, then put them in the detailed reporting duties. Guaranteed the assignment will be done to exacting standards of perfection. If you have Golden Retrievers on your team, you can ask them to do just about anything and they will do it out of loyalty to you, the way you want it done. If you need someone motivated invite the Otter along to play, but watch them as they may have a short attention span. And the Lions, well, they will make sure things get done, although you will want to watch the potential path of destruction behind them if they are an immature Lion!

People will thrive when they are in a position that matches their style. If you are unable to change their positions, then change some of their tasks to suit their style. You will begin to see them flourish and then the other areas of their work life will benefit as well. Here is a resource for further information on the animal model of leadership and personality styles *http://weirdblog.wordpress.com/2007/02/22/personality-types-lion-beaver-otter-and-golden-retriever/*

Communication Preferences

We all have our preferential way of communicating. Personally, I would much rather sit in front of you or talk to you on the phone than have a conversation through email. Whichever way suits you the best, do maintain a balance of face time, talk time and email. We are after all human beings. We need the human interaction and the benefit of facial expression, body language and tone of voice.

You may have someone who will only communicate to you through email. The reasoning behind that could be its anonymity and the desire to keep track of all communication for reference sake. Get them out of that comfort zone to talk to you on a regular basis either by phone or in person.

Some may be office door stalkers, waiting to speak to you about a simple issue or just say "Hi"! This will be destructive to your own focus on the projects you are working on. Studies have shown that after each distraction, it takes us nine minutes to return to the flow that we were in before we were distracted.

Having completed the second section of this workbook on *Minimalize Your Distractions*, you know the value of this concept and more than likely you have a great deal of time on your hands to think strategically and focus on your work. Set up some boundaries for the person who wants your face-to-face attention by asking them to send an email before stopping by, you can then respond with a time that is beneficial for the both of you.

Find out what each person, including your manager, prefers as a communication preference and then find a good balance that works for you and the team.

Extrinsic Motivators

These are of great importance in building relationships is to know what motivates everyone around you. Here are a couple of motivators:

- A day off or compensatory time

- Dress down day

- Longer lunch
- Attending a training course
- Financial bonuses or rewards
- Shopping or gas cards
- Public recognition
- Food
- Time with you!
- Being put on a special project
- Given more responsibility
- Company recognition programs with a point structure

Each person is different and what may float one person's boat may sink another's. Many of us have experienced the recognition reward when your manager asks you to come down to the front of the room. They tell gloating stories of your achievements and excellence while you stand there not hearing a word they say because you are dying from embarrassment inside wanting to run out of the room screaming! Too bad those reward givers didn't know that they were not rewarding, but torturing you into a deep dark hole of embarrassment. Many of us, on the other hand, love that type of recognition, we thrive, make jokes up front and smile broadly as the trophy is handed to us.

Know each person's preference. If you don't know, you must find out? Ask. They will tell you. Write a list of motivators, like the ones I have written above and have each individual make check marks by the ones they prefer. It is a simple and certain way to answer the question.

Intrinsic Motivators

For generations we have indeed motivated extrinsically with either the carrot or the stick; the stick being fear, the carrot being reward. We now know that the results with this type of motivation are limited in many ways.

We find that extrinsic motivation works very well with people who are in jobs of repetition where their need to be creative is limited. For those who are the problem-solvers and creative thinkers, the way to see them explode in their day-to-day achievements is to motivate them intrinsically.

My friend *Paul Herr*, released his book in 2009 entitled *Primal Management*. Paul's brilliant approach to employee engagement is to look at the five (5) social appetites of a human being. Herr looks at the psychological and biological keys to motivating employees, which are:

1. **The Cooperation Appetite**: merging individuals into a cohesive organism

2. **The Competency Appetite**: developing confident experts in each of your employees

3. **The Skill-Deployment Appetite**: designing a workplace that thrives on achievement and the thrill of a win

4. **The Innovation Appetite**: fostering an environment of innovation

5. **The Self-Protection Appetite**: understanding how people want and need to be protected

Paul helps us to understand what it takes to create an environment of fully functioning, intrinsically motivated human beings in the workplace. I can also tell you that he created a fabulous, simple and inexpensive tool to help us measure these motivations and our greatest assets, our people. The *Horsepower System* provides monthly measurements to see how the team is doing based on the five appetites and some ideas of how to change what we see in the results of that survey. I highly recommend having a read and a look at his work this month.

Clean My Tools

> *"Rather than focusing on things and time, focus on preserving and enhancing relationships and on accomplishing results."*
> *— Stephen Covey*

This month we have a great deal of "up-front" work to do. Once we get that done, we can begin to tweak the areas of concern. So let's begin with this:

Lunch

Who do you need to build your relationship with? Identify some points about yourself that are safe to share. If you are totally uncomfortable with this "lunch" idea, then begin with a practice lunch with someone who is less of a threat to you; someone you trust.

If you are not that shy, then set your appointments, make sure you tell them why you are taking them to lunch (to get to know them better) and don't talk about work. List the names and write topics you are comfortable sharing. Get them on your schedule.

Read a summary or purchase **Paul Herr's** book *Primal Management* it is an easy read and you will enjoy his approach. If you are interested in knowing more about Paul's *Horsepower Survey* to help you gauge where your biggest assets are intrinsically motivated, drop me an email at <u>horsepower@igniteachievements.com</u>. It is easy to set up, very cost effective and you can administrate it with ease.

Use this table to get to know the members of your team on a greater basis. Start with you and then your team. Here is an example:

Name		Holly
	What you think now	After asking them
Frequency	Low frequency	Low frequency
Personality	Lion – otter	Lion – golden retriever
Communication	Phone	Phone
Extrinsic motivator	Shopping cards	Compensatory time
Intrinsic motivator	Innovation	Innovation
Which area do I need to coach?	Frequency is too low. I need her to send me updates by email every other day.	
In the right job? If not what projects will engage personality more effectively?	Yes, Holly is in the right job and I think she has taken on way too much because of her golden retriever personality. I need to teach her how to delegate more effectively and how to say no more often so she doesn't get overwhelmed.	
What can I do to engage her intrinsic motivator?	Interest her to reengineer a process and work with Susan to write a detailed solution for the knowledge base.	

Deborah R. Monroe

This Chart is specifically for you!

Name	Me	
	What you think now	After thinking about it more in depth
Frequency		
Personality		
Communication		
Extrinsic motivator		
Intrinsic motivator		
Which area do I need to be coached?		
In the right job? If not what projects will engage my personality more effectively?		
What can I do to engage my intrinsic motivator?		

Permission to copy this page as many times as needed for your team.

Name		
	What you think now	After asking them
Frequency		
Personality		
Communication		
Extrinsic motivator		
Intrinsic motivator		
Which area do I need to coach?		
In the right job? If not what projects will engage personality more effectively?		
What can I do to engage their intrinsic motivator?		

Deborah R. Monroe

Maintenance

> *Treat people as if they were what they ought to be, and you help them to become what they are capable of being.* — Goethe

What did I discover about my people that I didn't know before I did the exercises earlier this month? Be detailed.

What information did I use to implement changes?

What changes, if any, have I seen in behavior and attitude? What are they?

Did I find Paul's book helpful? What specifically sparked my interest? Did I see yourself and my own motivators? What drives me and how can I make space for myself to enter into that motivation? What can I do for my people regarding their motivators?

Do I need to bring someone in to help reengage those motivators? What would the cost be? Where can I find the right person? When can I begin myself?

BLADE #7

Manage My Thought Life

"Gifted leadership occurs when heart and head—feeling and thought—meet. These are the two winds that allow a leader to soar — Daniel Goleman

As with the power of our words, so is the power of our thoughts. What goes on in our heads has so much power over us it is scary. It can drive a person mad or it can drive them to the greatest success and peace. In this month's section we will discuss what and how the thoughts in our head shape our world and affect those around us. Religions over the world; wise men from ages past have encouraged mankind to control their thoughts. They have suggested that if we humans can corral our thoughts we can corral the universe's explosive energy. Personally, I just want to manage my thoughts around eating chocolate! How can I do that? First I need to know who is talking to me!

The Voices In Your Head

We live in a sea of voices; waves crashing up onto the rocky shores of our consciousness. Sometimes the sea is calm and restful. A wind comes from one direction or another and then the storm begins raging. The water is stirred and everything that was at the bottom floats to the top in a mucky mix of pounding force.

Beyond the external distractions, beyond the needs of others pulling at our sleeve we must endure our own head, which is our biggest distraction. Our own self, the media or simply the things we have experienced over time can compound those thoughts.

We must determine what is going on by asking ourselves these simple questions:

- Is this true?
- Is this real, but not my truth?
- Is this a judgment?
- Is this someone else's expectation?
- Is this a past experience gone awry?
- Who's talking to me in my head?
- Is this an assumption?
- Is this a lie?

Being mindful enough to identify which of these is happening to you at one time takes energy and effort. So we will practice this at the end of the section. First, here are some brief definitions.

Is this true: is the thought in your head based on *fact* and on *truth* despite the emotion? There is a difference between fact and truth!

Is this real, but not my truth: is what I am hearing a real issue, yet it doesn't line up with my value or belief system?

Is this a judgment: is the thought based upon years of looking at this issue the same way?

Is this someone else's expectations: am I feeling pressure to think this way because another person expects me to?

Who is talking in my head: is this me? Or have I head it before and from whom?

Is this an assumption: am I listening to what I know is true, or am I creating "what if" scenarios?

Is this a lie: does this thought have any basis on what I know is true in fact or your faith?

Once we have established what the specific thought is that is tormenting or bothering us we can manage it more directly. When thoughts that are not truth stay hidden in the darkness, they get really big and scary. Bringing them out into the light by speaking them or discussing them helps their power to wane and thereby takes away their influence.

Let's spend some time reviewing who could be talking to us and how those voices influence our emotional reactions and our behaviors. If the question arises in your head, "am I hearing voices", the answer is quite simply, YES!

My Mother's voice: this one could go either way! I say this in jest, knowing that my mother will definitely read this book, so I will tread lightly! I hear my mother's voice all the time in my head. The mother of my youth says to me, "did you clean your room, did you brush your teeth, did you do the dishes?" This is a small sampling of the voice of my mother, which of course, comes in other ways, full of wisdom and discernment. She lives on! The funny thing is that my mom's *mother's* voice is as strong today as it was when she was a child. We often joke around about what Hannah (my grandmother) would say concerning specific situation and in what tone it would be said. We even go so far as to imitate her on occasion and then smile to ourselves about our brilliant ability to bring her back to life for a moment in time.

My Dad's voice: my dad has said so many things to me, some scary and some wise (as his wisdom to me about using a dull knife I shared with you in the beginning of this book). Yet, when I am troubled about my life and my future I always hear his voice speaking to me specifically from the kitchen of our split ranch style house in upstate New York when I was nine year old. He said, "Deborah, when you grow up, you can be anything you want to be and do anything you want to do, you are that smart." Ok, I might of added the "you are that smart" part, but I know that was, in essence, what he meant!

The Other Kids in School: I cannot tell you how much these voices influence me on a daily basis. I can say wholeheartedly that most of the voices I hear from my school days were 80% negative. One that rings out very loud is from a girl in 7th grade that came up to me while I was sitting down in a chair. She proceeded to pinch the skin that was falling over my hip-hugger pants and said with distain *"you are fat!"* I look back at pictures of my teen years with amazement seeing a slender and lean girl of 12 wondering to whom she was actually comparing me.

Those words come blaring back at me every time I get on a scale; every time I look in a mirror to study myself; every time I wake up in the morning having had a very salty meal the night before. I fight those words; I battle them sometimes to no avail. They shaped the assessment of my self to this day. I consistently push them around in my head, try to block them out and stand firm in loving myself, no matter what the scale says. It is an ongoing battle for life, one which I will eventually win, fat or not, I refuse to let those words affect the person I have become today and will become in the future.

The negative voices of Others: there are many people in my life who have negative things to say about me, whether those things are true or not, it doesn't matter, they still stick in my head and cause me to question myself, my intentions and my actions. I had one person say that I was "too bubbly". After years of suppressing my "bubble", I finally decided, that was a lie and if I was a "bubble" then I better go out and start floating around.

Those words affected me deeply and changed my behavior. I shut that part of me down as I was led to believe that it was not appropriate. Once I did a little self-inventory and realized that being "bubbly" was part of who I was and how that aspect of my personality came to be, I squashed the lie and allowed myself to be authentic. Darn them if they can't take a good bubble!

I think the underlying message from them is that they were jealous that I could so easily thrive and fit in around any situation with any person in any environment. I began the "bubble" at the young age of one year to my mother's horror. I would go up to anyone and start a conversation.

The Boss' voice: ah, this one can haunt you until you die, depending upon the types of managers that you have experienced over the years. I have both wonderful and alternatively hair-raising experiences with bosses' voices and often hear both voices screaming in my head. I hear the *"Deborah, you are a maverick. You do know what a maverick is, don't you? It's a horse that is wild and won't submit. You need to be corralled."* This manager's voice makes me laugh now. But at the time I trembled thinking that there was something so drastically wrong with me that I would never make anything of my world or myself. The wonderful thing about this statement is that I have lived up to that manager's expectations in every way. I thank God on every occasion, for creating me to be a maverick. It is a much more exciting life for me than running around a corral in circles all day!

Another manager's voice I hear on a regular basis as well. This manager always treated me with great respect and empowerment. Although we learn very well from negative inferences like the above mentioned, we also learn very well from kindness and being valued. I learned how to deal with people by not only what she taught me, but how she made me feel at the end of every day. Her voice is gentle and calm, encouraging and merciful. I react best to that type of voice. If you want to get me to do something, this is the best approach for me.

My Own voice: many times we are harder on ourselves than anyone else could ever be. No matter where the judgments come from or where the expectations come from, I know one thing for sure. I need to speak nicely to myself. With all the other voices influencing how I think about one thing or another; with all the crazy ideas and media frenzy that pours into us every day, I am the only one that can say to myself, "Deborah, everything is going to be okay." I speak to myself, sometimes out loud (when no one is around), I encourage myself, I tell myself that what I have to give to myself and others is of great worth; that the work I do is powerful and meaningful. I may not have had the original thought or done the massive quantities of research that others have done, but using their work I continue to have my own unique perspective and human experience that makes my voice a powerful one.

I am no long squashed by other's expectations of my "bad" behavior. I am no longer under their influence, I have found my voice and what I have to say to myself and others brings relief and life. This is what I hope for, concerning you.

I hope that you find your voice and make it heard. Tell you partner, your manager, your peers, your direct reports, your children, your friends, your parents, the unproductive voices still bouncing around in your head, and perhaps even the heavens themselves what you have to say and who you are. Let the words ring right out of your mouth and let them be seasoned, as it were, with salt (a preservative). Let your voice and words be filled with kindness, truth, understanding, and wisdom. Let you voice be your own and let it be unique in the world as you are.

Deborah R. Monroe

Awfulizing or Vain Imaginings

Once we begin to recognize the types of thoughts going through our minds and "who" is speaking these thoughts to us through our memories, it will become much easier to identify this behavior of awfulizing or what I call *vain imaginings*.

Capturing *vain imaginings* is a practice that is very difficult to manage. Some common terms we use for this type of behavior are: worrywart, fussbudget or fusspot, doomsayer, pessimist, and prophet of doom! As far as I can see with my research, the word "worrywart" arrived around 1935 into our language.

They all point to the same meaning, which in essence means that we create all types of different scenarios in our heads around "what if's". We look for a threat and we find what we are looking for. We list eight possibilities and become certain it is about two or three of those possibilities. Then we focus on just one. The ONE thought becomes the absolute truth. Our behavior then aligns with what is in our heads and voilà, we surprise everyone with our reaction.

Most of the time that ONE thought is wrong in its assumption, thank goodness. But when that ONE thought is right, we let people know about it by loudly pronouncing, "I knew I was right, I saw this coming" or "I told you so!"

The problem exists in the amount of time and energy we spend creating these scenarios or vain imaginings because they are based upon limited information of what is happening now; they are based on pre conceived notions and they are based upon what happened in our experiences of the past.

I struggle with this one as we all do. I have friends who live in torment with this every day. And, when I say torment, I mean that their thinking patterns are so used to playing this game that it causes them excessive chemical imbalance with all the adrenaline and cortisol the brain pumps into their systems. The effects of that overflowing chemical mixture causes them much angst, hyper sensitivity to things that people say and do; poisons their liver and kidneys, plays havoc with their ability to sleep, erodes their brain neurons and plays tricks with their ability to see what is really happening and overcome the situation because of fear.

It is, in a couple of words, the brain's folly and creates a totally unproductive living space.

One of my favorite examples to share around this subject is this. Let's say that you are at home. Your partner is late coming home from work. They were due back about 20 minutes ago. Here is the brain's ongoing conversation with you, follow it closely, here we go:

"Ah geez, why are they late? I hope they are ok...

I bet they got stuck in traffic, yeah, that's it, I better turn the radio on to see if there was an accident on the highway".

Five minutes go by...

"I can't imagine where they are! They are never this late home. I wonder... oh, I hope they weren't in an accident, oh my God, oh God no...where did I put the number to the hospital. If they are not home in 15 minutes I am going to call the hospital. Or would the hospital have called me? Why didn't they call, they have a cell phone...no, they are probably stuck in traffic; everything is going to be fine. Well, you know, I *did* catch them winking at the new person at work, you don't suppose....no, they would never do that...but....**that** new person was very good looking....they can't be having an affair...they would not dare....wait a minute...they left this morning in a mood and didn't kiss me goodbye...well that (expletive)...I can't believe that after all these years they would go and do that...I knew this was coming. This is why they looked at me that way the other day." (expletive)...(mumbling under the breath)...

In walks the partner after a long day at work, "Hi honey, I am home!"

Response, "You!!!...you (expletive)...I want a flipping divorce; you can't cheat on me and get away with it. I want you out of here right now......."

It is a nutty scenario, but you know what, this type of thing goes through our heads all the time. Scenarios are created; we react and behave according to what is happening in our heads. It takes a great deal of practice to weed out the scenarios and wait until we have all the information we need to create the right decisions and reactions. If we practice that, not only will our health improve, but all the relationships around us will as well.

Practice this yourself, but also be aware that those around you including your employees, peers, managers, family and friends have these same reactions in their brains. If you ask one of your team members to come and see you for a meeting, or go to lunch with you, you can bet dollars to donuts that their brains are going to start playing with the reason of "why" you are asking to meet with them. Rumors, rumors of wars and wars themselves have begun with less.

So manage the people around you by not only telling them when you want to talk to them, but what it is about and why you want to speak with them. Keep their minds on their work and projects, not in torment thinking that they are headed to the "principle's office'.

Judging Others

We judge situations and people most of the day, every day. Our brains look predominantly for negatives over 75% of the time to keep us safe. Our eyes scan, the ears perk, and the nose sniffs. Concerning this, the only difference between animals and us is that we take in that information and filter it through our cognitive minds. Much judging during our day has to do with poor listening skills, dislikes or expectations of others and ourselves. It can also be tied in nicely with "jumping to conclusions"!

There is an intangible essence of energy that happens when we judge others and ourselves.

Consider that you are the driver in a car. You stop. Someone you know gets into the passenger seat. This passenger has a judgment on you. They think that you are a lousy driver. All of a sudden, what would have been an easy drive becomes hindered. You are more self-conscious. You may hit a garbage can or cross the double yellow line, stop short on several occasions. What ever happened, you noticed a marked difference in your driving ability, and it doesn't get better. You stop and let the passenger out of the car and with that simple act of letting them out of your car; your driving becomes "normal" again. Your confidence returns and off you go.

Another example is the judgment that of a particular person who has the tendency to always be late for any event they are invited to. You tell them to come an hour early knowing that they will come an hour late. Even if this person leaves on or before time, chances are that the judgments on them are going to have some wild affect that cause every red light, every slow truck and accident to occur as they are making their way to your event. It is like a self-fulfilling prophecy. You get what you expect!

Honestly, I don't know the science or phenomenon behind how this works. What I can say is that it does affect us, to whatever level. If someone is expected to act or behave in the way we believe, they will. What ever the energy of a judgment is, it impacts us and makes us behave differently. A judgment puts our behavior in a box that we seemingly cannot get out of and it takes a great deal of energy and self-awareness to escape them. That is how judgments affect us.

What can we do about the judgments that others have on us or that we self-impose? Listen. Listen deeply and ask yourself why am I responding this way? Did I want to behave like this? Was this my intention or is it something else? Here are some common judgments that may affect all of us and also some you want to "listen" for internally: When you are with a specific person or group of people do you find:

- You always feel "stupid"
- You always eat too much
- When you go to their house, you are always late, no matter what
- You tend to control things when you had no intention to do so
- You stumble with your words
- You cannot make a decision
- You never call them when you are supposed to
- You live up to whatever their expectations are of you!

Those are just a few. As you listen this month you are to identify the judgments that you hear against you. Once those judgments have been found out, you will work on acknowledging them and when you are with the people who have these expectations create a strategy that will prove them wrong.

Another way that judgments attached themselves to us is through our lack of listening skills, which I imagine have much improved since you completed that section in this workbook.

We have the propensity to gather these judgments at work. We all have people we like better than other people at the office. Let's say a person we like comes into our office and complains to us about one of the people we don't like as well. We can usually snap to a decision about the unfortunate soul and create a solution of how we are going to handle that person or situation in our head. Our behavior then changes towards that person in question and we become gruff or short with them. All this is done in a thoughtless manner and we do it without even finding out what their side of the story is.

The key here is to inhibit our reaction until both sides of a story have been told. This is harder than it seems because of our brain. Our brain loves to jump to conclusions. There are well-worn neural pathways, similar to hiking trails in the woods. The electricity runs down them smoothly with no limits or stop signs. At the chance of seeming silly, I will share one of my foibles of jumping to a conclusion with you.

I visited a new hair stylist a while back. There were only two chairs in the salon in the back of a clothing store. When I walked in, I saw a woman with long thick auburn hair sitting in the other chair. She didn't talk, although I knew she was listening to my conversation with my stylist. She was getting her hair dyed and had the warming lights in a red glow over her head. As I was settling in, I glanced over and saw her profile. I thought to myself, she is the most unattractive woman I have seen in a long time. She had a big nose and a very small chin. I looked at her clothing and saw she had probably just come from working and more than likely that was working with horses or on a ranch, because she had big dirty work boots on with jeans tucked into them. I then turned back to my business, but on occasion, I turned to her and my thought process began again. It was soon time for her to get up and have the dye rinsed out. And as she rose, in our close quarters, I realized that this was no woman. She in fact was a man with long locks. I was embarrassed and ashamed of myself. I had fallen quite unintentionally into assuming something that was totally incorrect because of the locale I was visiting. The interesting part to me was that not only was this judgment glaring at me like a rotten tomato, showing me what needed to be looked at in my own self, but that I fell into it so unabashedly and unaware.

We are all vulnerable to this type of thinking, of judging others. I hope you find those judgments this month before they show up and talk very loudly in an accusatory fashion and get you in trouble! All judgments and criticisms are a tragic expression of an unmet need within.

Forgiveness

All the things we have spoken of in this section have power over us; some, healthy power, some unhealthy. It is the unhealthy thought patterns, voices and judgments that we will consider now. In whatever way these things are disquieting to us, by making us act in ways that we have and in ways that we had no intention of acting. Forgiveness needs to be considered as a method of change and releasing these actions or reactions.

First, forgiveness is for YOU, to give or receive. The act of saying, "I forgive you", may or may not release the other person, yet it will release you. I am not sure where I stand on seeking out apologies. I don't know if it is appropriate or not. I do know that it is nice to think that someone values and cares about us enough to seek forgiveness and say they are sorry. But, that is about them, not about you.

There seems to be a power beyond the natural in forgiveness. There is a release that instruments a new beginning and freedom. Let us begin with what forgiveness is and what it is not.

Forgiveness is not bending someone to your will; it is not about exacting revenge, it may or many not come with a feeling when given or received. Asking forgiveness also doesn't mean that we forget what happened.

What I do find forgiveness to be is one or both of these things:

1. A decision to forgive – a cognitive choice

2. A true understanding and association of what another was thinking, feeling or the reasons they were acting a specific way.

The Mayo Clinic has found that when forgiveness is present, so is quicker healing and mental rest to the human being. There are insurmountable studies that prove the same thing. If you hold resentment, bitterness and unforgiveness, it poisons you inside and out; it poisons relationships and stunts their growth. There is nothing uglier than bitterness, which grows untamed and unhindered in the garden of unforgiveness. There is something about bitterness that turns the stomach; it breeches all attempts at peace and reconciliation. It wreaks havoc with productivity at work and relationships in every area of our lives.

To forgive is to understand and realize that the other person was doing the best they could with what they had at the time.

To ask for forgiveness is a humble act of admitting that your actions, words, deed or internal processes were not life giving or charitable. To ask is difficult. Especially if you are asking with no expectations of receiving a "yes, I forgive you," comment.

In my younger years, I felt like a bull in a china shop. I thought I should write a book with that title to share all the stories of myself bumping into people and breaking things within and around them. I learned quickly that to sustain relationships, the ability to ask someone to forgive you, with humility and sincerity, was paramount. I think I got to the point where I was practicing this on a daily basis because I would blow it with someone every seeming moment.

There was an older lady who was an acquaintance. She seemed to me to be very intrusive and pithy. At one point of many, I offended her, which was not a difficult task in my mind. Yet, I offended her nevertheless. I sat one evening in the hallway next to phone piecing my words together as I knew I needed to deal with the situation. My heart was racing, my mouth dry as I dialed her number. Upon her answering the phone, my breath got short and I gasped. My mind went blank and I stumbled to get the words out of my mouth. "I understand that you are upset with me and I have called to ask you to forgive me for what I did to upset you". In saying that simple phrase, I felt such a relief. But then came her response, which I did not expect…or maybe I did. "Well, that's just fine. You can ask forgiveness if you want to, but it doesn't change a thing. You have been a (expletive).. and a (another expletive)….. And as far as I can tell you will always be a (you know what)…..so NO I don't forgive you." Stunned and speechless, I quietly said, "I am sorry you feel that way, I called to ask you to forgive me and tell you I was sorry. Bye".

I hung up the phone in shock, heart still pumping too fast and very hurt. That was the first time that one of my apologies had been met with refusal. I knew that my own heart was clear. I did what I felt was right and she would have to be reminded of her anger towards me until she decided to accept that apology.

We will always make mistakes. The most honorable thing we can do is accept responsibility for our actions. For others, we can accept their regrets and create a place for them in that apology.

What happens when we do not forgive when something has been done to us? How does it hinder us?

Jack was just that person. When I began to coach Jack there was a sense that not all was right in his world. Although promised one position, he was doing another, which was a demotion, he thought. His managers were totally fed up with his destructive behavior. He was controlling, mean and angry, yet they kept him around for his technical knowledge. This happens a great deal in corporate environments; tornado like behavior slides because the person has such a vast amount of technical, process or business knowledge. If I do anything with this story, please let it create the awareness within you that you will stop the bleeding before it gets worse.

Back to Jack: Jack was to all intents and purposes innocent of all wrongdoing, as per his comments. It was his management that was at fault for putting him in this situation. Understanding of their point of view, forgiveness for their actions towards him was far from reality, his reality. His coaching should have begun 10 years before, but in a last ditch effort to save him the mangers chose to finally invest in some guidance. Jack's issue is that he would not and could not forgive anything. He constantly blamed others for his demise, however unfair it was, it was their fault. He could not see that the unforgiveness in his heart was destroying any chance he had of keeping his job or thriving in a way that was productive to him and his company. That victim mentality continues to be a scourge on our energy and creativity. When we find someone blaming others for their lease on life, hurt is at the surface, unforgiveness is at the heart and bitterness is at the root. With all authenticity, I too fell into this blaming attitude in a couple of jobs I held. It was not a pretty sight. I did this until I realized it really was time for me to go and that I no longer needed to be a victim for which I was blaming them. Freedom is dear and always hard won.

Marshal Rosenberg, as mentioned previously, made a statement at one of his conferences that I attended. *"When someone becomes angry with you, it means that they don't see you as human until you have met their standards"*. Now who is playing God?

Consider this when you get angry as well - when you get angry, just sit back and enjoy the horror show in your own head! Listen to what you head is going through. Determine to empathetically connect with what is alive in you and what need was not met inside. When we do that, forgiveness of ourselves and others will come much quicker and we can get back to the business at hand instead of frothing all over our lives with rabid intent and hurt that has turned into anger.

Since I regard forgiveness as empathy in it's purist form we need to understand that as **Daniel Goleman** in his book *Emotional Intelligence: Why It Can Matter More Than IQ* states, "people's emotions are rarely put into words; far more often they are expressed through other cues. Just as the mode of the rational mind is words, the mode of the emotions is nonverbal." **Daniel Pink**, one of my favorite authors and speakers mentions in his book, *A Whole New Mind, Why Right Brainers Will Rule the Future*, expresses so well, "The main canvas for displaying those emotions is the face. With forty-three tiny muscles that tug and stretch and lift our mouth, eyes, cheeks, eyebrows and forehead, our faces can convey the full range of human feeling. Since empathy depends on emotion and since emotion is conveyed nonverbally, to enter another's heart, you must begin the journey by looking into his face."

That last sentence struck a deep resounding cord within me. To ask for or to give forgiveness is not something that should be done thru email or texting or even on the phone. It is the human face to face, eye-to-eye interaction that brings about the relationship building. It is not for cowards or those who shrink back. Like the *Valiant Conversation*, forgiveness requires a bold heart that settles its sights on something more exclusive in our existence. And whatever that is, it is honorable and courageous. It makes me a better person inside; it makes you a better person inside and it makes those around us better for being with us. Consider the power of making the commitment and connection of forgiveness so that we can move on with our lives, in our health and so that others can do the same.

Deborah R. Monroe

Clean My Tools

> *"We cannot rise higher than our thought of ourselves."*
> *— Orison Swett Marden*

> *"What this power is I cannot say; all I know is that it exists and it becomes available only when a man is in that state of mind in which he knows exactly what he wants and is fully determined not to quit until he finds it."*
> *— Alexander Graham Bell*

This month was all about you, your head and your heart. We have a great deal to consider, so let's get to work.

Who is talking and what are they saying?

State	Who is it?	How does it make you feel	What are your actions to quiet it?
Is this true?			
Is this real, but not my truth?			
Is this a judgment?			
Is this someone else's expectation?			
Is this a past experience gone awry?			
Who's talking to me in my head?			
Is this an assumption?			
Is this a lie?			

What subjects do I end up awfulizing about on a continuous basis?

What was the last vain imagining I let my brain create?

What can I do for my staff or family to help them stop awfulizing?

Deborah R. Monroe

Identify common judgments that you have. Who are they against? What do they sound like and what should you do about it?

Name	What are they?	What strategy can I create to lessen them?
Karice	I think she always looks for mistakes in my work	Have a conversation with her about how I feel she does that and ask her if it true. And if it is, have someone check my work before I give it to her.

Who do I need to ask forgiveness from? Write down any names that come to mind without judging the situation or thinking about how you will do it. Write down the emotions that come up when you think each one.

Name	Situation	Emotions

What could a likely outcome be if I do not ask these people to forgive me? How could it affect me personally? My job? My family? My relationships?

When am I going to schedule these conversations? What do I need to do for myself to prepare?

Who do I need to forgive for their action against me?

Name	Situation	Emotions

Deborah R. Monroe

What could a likely outcome be if I do not forgive these people? How could it affect me personal? My job? My family? My relationships? My health?

When am I going to schedule these conversations? What do I need to do for myself to prepare?

Maintenance

> *It is not enough to be busy; so are the ants. The question is: what are we busy about?* — Henry David Thoreau

I imagine this was a challenging month with the tasks that you embraced. My hopes are that you were able to speak to your coach or accountability partner about what you discovered and the actions you took.

Let's review:

Who was talking the loudest in your head? Was it a truth or a lie? What have you done to inhibit or take action concerning that voice?

Did you discover your own voice? What is it that you said to those around you?

Your parents:

Your partner?

Your children?

_____

Your co-workers?

_____

Your manager?

_____

The heavens?

_____

Yourself?

_____

Anyone else?

_____

What were the results of being able to speak your truth?

_____

_____

_____

What was the biggest revelation about your vain imaginings? How have you been able to manage your head concerning these? What work is left to create more freedom in your mind?

On a scale from 1-10 how judgmental were you in the beginning of the month? What about now? What made the difference?

When you made the effort to ask others to forgive you, what was their response? Have you noticed a change in your relationships since then?

When you made the effort to forgive others for what they have done to you what happened in your own head? Were you able to understand why they did what they did and extend empathy and mercy to them?

How has forgiving others affected you this month?

BLADE #8

Let Go And Delegate

"Carve your name on hearts and not on marble."
— *Charles Spurgeon*

There are so many reasons that we keep our work close to our chest. When I say close to our chest, I mean, holding on by means of control or the inability to delegate. In emotional intelligence terms we measure this in levels of adaptability and flexibility. Over the many years of coaching people who have "suffered" under this controlling aspect of their personality and those that have suffered under them, I want us to explore the some of the reasons why we create this environment either willingly or by default. It is of utmost importance that you understand that all humans have the same needs. We simply have developed different strategies to handle those needs and to meet them.

We are so controlling and therefore become overwhelmed with the amount of work that we must do because we refuse to delegate even the simplest of tasks. The unfortunate result of that type of action is that I have found that managers and executives find themselves doing 80% operational work and limiting their ability to think and act strategically to 20% of their time. In these types of positions we need the advantage of having more time to build our organizations with at least 60% strategic concentration and 40% operational attention. But how do we offload that work and maintain sanity?

Steven represents a multitude of people that I have worked with over the years. They were either in the office next door or on the phone with me being coached. Steven has the tendency to tell people what to do. And usually, it is done with a firm, no nonsense tone of voice that is demanding and cool. Steven doesn't really care about how you feel about the task being assigned to you. He doesn't really look at you as a human being; he looks at you as a "human-doing". We are here to get a job done and do it well. He is not really liked for being himself, rather Steven is feared and bowed down to…probably "yes'ed" to death. Disaster in his organization is lurking below the surface. His employees are not committed, they are more like slaves of the paycheck, biding their time until another opportunity arises that will free them from Steven's chains and give them a greater opportunity to be creative, be listened to and valued.

Where does this need to control come from? Where does the need to have our hands in every piece of the pie come from? How can we really expect to get anything done if we are so desperate to control every aspect of the business? With attitudes like this, we end up being operational, in every aspect. We give ourselves no space to think about the future with our fingerprints all over the present. How then can you be strategic, which is what they pay you to do?

Let's dive a little more into the depth of control. Steven controls because he doesn't want to look bad to his superiors. He wants to make sure that all his "ducks" are in a row. He does not want to be caught off guard and embarrassed. So, he has to make sure that everything around him supports his agenda and keeps him off the hot seat. He barks his orders, throws looks of distain at his peers and direct reports and basically makes everyone's life miserable…but he doesn't care because he is getting the job done right! Or so he thinks!

It is really important to know that behavior is driven by your emotions. When someone acts out, there is an emotion in the background pushing that behavior.

It is also very important, to realize that emotions are driven by needs. Meaning, emotions of joy and contentment are driven by met needs; emotions of fear, anger, hurt, and the like are driven by un-met needs.

I speak for myself first, knowing that I have indeed been challenged in this area in my past and sometimes present. I admit this with no shame, as I have learned to understand why I fall into this pattern and then understood with enough self-awareness that I need to check myself if I am not to fall back into old patterns of behavior.

The early rigidity of my personality came handed down from my neural architects, namely parental influence. In my early twenties I completed a Myers Briggs personality analysis and mostly scored a high "J" (judging), which was surprising to me as I had always been the opposite. The "J" person chooses closure and everything needs to be in its proper place. J's are settled, decided, fixed, plan ahead, and structured. I say this to give you a little greater understanding of what I "suffer" with! Two of my family members are high "P's" (perceiving). That means they are very flexible, open, spontaneous and unstructured, which drives "J's" crazy! Instead of being driven crazy, I pursue peace and growth and therefore, I have to add more "perceiving" into my own person in order to keep aligned and thriving in the relationship. In laymen's terms, I need to pick my battles and let the rest go!

Many years ago, I was in charge of administrating a cassette tape ministry. I would take the orders, count the money, create the labels, copy the tapes, categorize and use my library science skills to make sure that the catalog of master tapes were all numbered and ordered correctly and put into correct place on the wall mounted storage rack. It would be late in the evening before I began filling orders. Each order would take about 7 minutes to copy, label, box and address. I found myself totally unable to leave the "tape room" until every order was complete and all things were put back in their proper place. Even if someone ran to me yelling that the building was burning down, I would not leave my post. I think that was one of the first times I had a self-actualization. I was being "controlled" by this obsessive desire to have everything in order. Why? I only guessed that everything else was so stressful and out of place in my life at the time, that this is the only time I felt in control and safe.

So here are some observations as to why we choose to control and over structure projects, relationships and life. It is helpful to know them, yet it does not help us to change. We will explore how to change this behavior later in this section:

I control or over structure things because:

- I want to be seen as the "go-to" guy/gal

- I want to look "competent" to my managers and those around me

- If you want something done right you need to do it yourself

- I don't trust others (my team, my relationship)

- I don't know how to be any other way

- I don't want to be ashamed or embarrassed by other's mistakes representing me?

- Everything else around me is out of control. I can control this area

- I don't want to make mistakes and show that I am vulnerable or weak

Most of these are *fear*-based behaviors. Fear of failure, fear of shame, fear of looking stupid, fear that someone else will be more successful, fear of being fired, fear that I will not keep the respect of others and lastly, fear of not having my needs met.

Not having needs met is a big motivator for all of humanity. So in order to meet those needs, we will in essence make sure to manipulate situations, control outcomes and in every way, make sure that we are not left making the mistakes that could be the motivators that create growth within us. Although uncomfortable, allowing ourselves to make mistakes is one of the greatest opportunities for us to learn. There is no shame in that at all!

Lawrence was a director that I worked with. His company came to me wanting to change his behavior of control. Their observation was that he was so controlling and so unwilling to be flexible in the changing times of the company that he needed to change or they would have to let him go. After his 360 assessment was done, it revealed that one of his lowest competencies was adaptability/flexibility, which in this case was hurting him and his entire organization. Lawrence and I had a heart to heart. I asked him why he felt he needed to control everything in his path. The answer came as a revelation to him. He had started at the company 20 years before, when he felt that he did not know anything. In order to cover the insecurity that people would find out that he didn't know anything he began to bark orders and control what could have been chaos around him.

I asked Lawrence if, after 20 years, he felt that he currently knew what he was doing. His answer was "Of course! I know this business inside and out!" So the realization came, now he *did* know the business, processes, and products, why was he still using a pattern of behavior that he had employed 20 years before when he didn't feel as confident? Lawrence did not have to protect that vulnerable part of himself any longer. He was an expert using a tactic of a novice because of conditioning. I heard the coin drop in Lawrence's head. He got it! That was when we began to explore the reason why he chose to keep that pattern of behavior and unravel the ropes that had entangled him and kept him bound to react the same way every time.

If you do not consider yourself a control-freak, ask someone to give you honest feedback about the subject. Know and remember that if your response is an emotion of defensiveness, then there may be something there that you honestly want to review within yourself. If you are ultimately very flexible and adaptable, we all know that there is always room for improvement, growth and greater understanding that will create a more productive life and work place. So dig in to this section just as deeply as someone who does struggle with the need to control.

Trust

With all of us who tend towards control one of the factors of "why" we do this is because we do not trust. We do not trust our partner, our bosses or perhaps even the people on our teams. They may have even proven us correct to not trust them.

We all come to the table with one of two levels of trust; natural trust or trust that needs to be earned. My father was one who had a point structure of trust. If I did something to earn his trust, I got two points. If I did something to disappoint that trust, I lost two points. Whether or not that was helpful to me, I saw his perspective and what was important to him. I am not sure how that has affected the way that I perceive trusting those around me, yet I can tell you that I don't use the measuring system!

I know that it is important to have a hard look at why we do or do not trust. I could say that hurt and fear are the emotions that rise to the top. Judgments and perceptions of how people treat us rise to the top of the pile in our minds. Experiences of the past and betrayal are big devourers of what is in the trust bucket.

On a personal note, one of my relationships of the past is an interesting case study along those lines. **Daniel** (name changed, obviously), and I entered into a relationship. His past woes' and experiences in relationships sited that all his other girlfriends cheated on him and were sneaky. He was convinced that every woman would do the same thing. Since I was always on the road and traveling a great deal, the opportunity for me to engage in that type of "hurtful" behavior was clearly possible in his mind. I could say for myself that engaging in that type of behavior was not part of my value and belief system. It wasn't until Daniel really knew my heart and my intention that he admittedly realized he was safe from harm. There was no question that it would ever be a problem.

Ryan, the CEO of an organization I worked with, the same type of trust issue came into play. I started to receive numerous calls about a client that Ryan wanted me to sell more products to; more of his products. I felt the pressure in his voice every time we spoke on the phone. He wanted to invite himself to the client site to help me convince the client that they needed more. The situation was very precarious to begin with because the client was in the middle of big organization restructuring, my main contacts where in flux and there was no knowing what the outcome would be. Still Ryan was very forceful, controlling in his speech and necessity for action. I was so uncomfortable with that approach that I wanted to hang up. Yet, being the concerned person, I am, I wanted to understand what was motivating that behavior in Ryan. I wanted to get to the root cause of why he would not let go of his forceful barragement. Then I asked quietly, "Ryan, do you trust me?" His reaction took him by surprise. "Deborah...I never thought of it that way. I do trust you". And when he said that, all of his angst, all of the verbal volley back and forth and his need to control the situation stopped like someone on the edge of a cliff, dramatically and completely. He was able to trust my intention. Trust that I was going to do everything I could to help us both but know that I had inside information about the political environment that needed to be considered as we moved cautiously around the pitfalls and hidden agendas that were surfacing in that company. Ryan knew that I understood his need.

What happens when trust, which is an empathetic expression and respect of another person, enters the picture? There is a physical feeling that the tension has gone from the situation or the person stops talking or slows down because they feel heard. In this case, Ryan felt heard and the tension dissipated instantly.

Trust is having confidence in someone or building their confidence in you.

How is that done? By stating your intention; by letting your words be your bond; by letting your actions speak even louder than your words. If others do not trust you, ask yourself why. Take a serious look at what wounding may have occurred either by your own hand or by someone else who was in your same position. Understand that if their experience was hurtful or they felt betrayed, it will take your effort to show them that it is okay to open themselves up again and trust.

If you are the one who does not trust, take a look at what you need to feel trust again and have that Valiant Conversation that speaks authentically and truthfully to the person who you lack trust in. It needs to be dealt with and it needs to be brought out into the light. Remember, if it stays in the dark it gets bigger, uglier and more concrete in its appearance.

Creating An Action Plan

Okay, so you want to let go of control and you want to learn how to trust or have people trust you. So how do we do that? Let's concentrate on what you can do to improve this at work if you are afraid to delegate.

We know that just asking someone to do something for you and delegating a responsibility is not going to calm the control monster in your head. We will take baby steps to offload some of the stress of doing this. One of the exercises that worked well with some of my coachees of the past has been this.

1. Pick a "C" list project that is not of the greatest importance. Something that if it doesn't get done perfectly will not hurt you or your organization.

2. Define to whom you want to delegate that project.

3. Create a list of action items that need to be completed around that project. The list will include who is responsible for each action item, the resources they will use and the time frame for the completion of each action item.

4. Tell the lucky person that you are learning how to delegate and taking your hands out of the pie in order to spend more time in strategic planning for your department

5. Tell that person that since you are in a learning curve yourself, you would like to have them check in with you at the end of each day to share their progress. This meeting is for you. It will build your confidence in the other person's ability, settle your fears and ensure that the person in charge of that project is on track within your expectations.

6. Once that person has proven to you that they are able and your "trust points" have been handed out approach them with another project on the "b" list or do steps 1 thru 5 with another person on your team.

As time progresses, you will find that you are changing the rules. Perhaps every action, resource or time line item will not need to be listed, perhaps at the end of every day you will not need a progress report. When that happens, trust is being built. And as you relieve yourself of more tasks, your time will open up and can be given to the much needed planning for your organization's success. The other amazing benefit of doing this is that you are teaching your team how to carefully fulfill expectations, problem solve and troubleshoot on their own. You are also managing your own fears and learning to grow by stepping out little by little. Good for you!

PS…You may or may not want to try this at home!

Clean My Tools

> *"Stay committed to your decisions, but stay flexible in your approach."* — *Anthony Robbins*

I am excited for each of us this month as we explore the issues of control and what is holding us in that pattern that may not be serving us well any longer.

Do this exercise for the week. Every time you need to control something, make a note of what it is in the first column. Look at what you were thinking when it happened in the second column. In the third column identify what emotion you were feeling. In the fourth, figure out what need was not being met or was being threatened. In the fifth column write down to whom you could have delegated that item.

Check the appendix for a list of human needs to help you identify them.

Event	What was I thinking?	What was I feeling?	What need was being threatened?	Who could I have delegated this to?
Project x	I don't want anyone else to get the credit for this.	Fear	My need to feel safe	Susan

Deborah R. Monroe

Fill in your trust circle. Start in the middle, the small circle and identify whom you trust implicitly with every aspect of your life and then move outward.

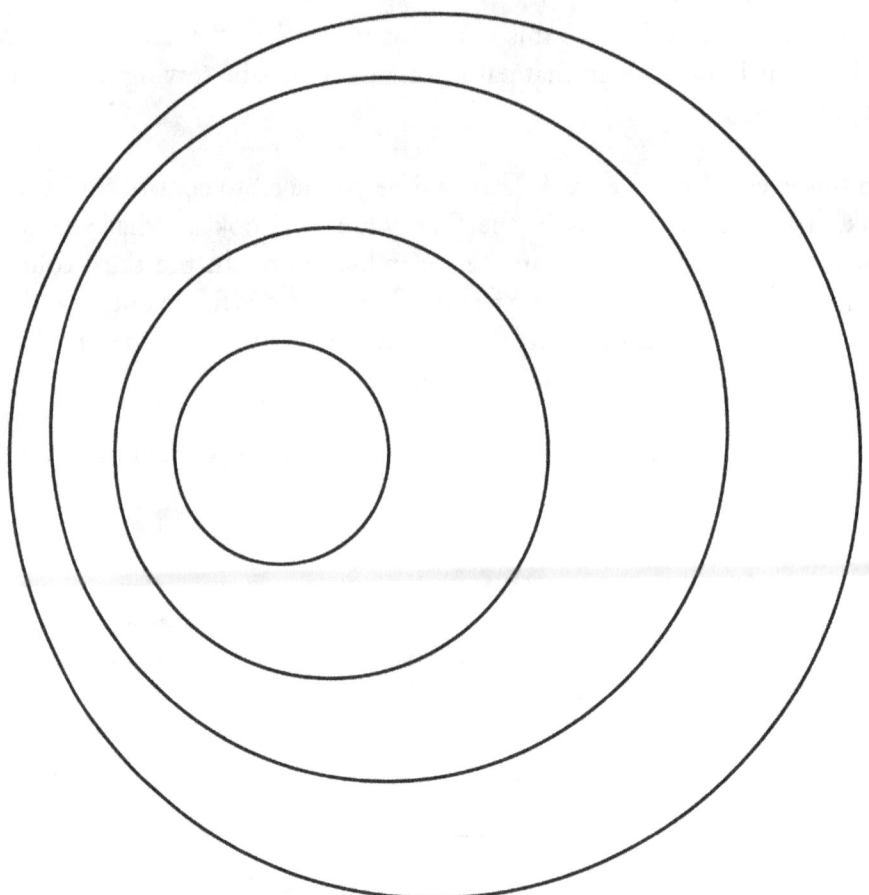

Take note of how many people are in your "inner circle". If there is only one or two, that is great! If there is no one in the inner circle, then this should give you something to work on over this next month. You will identify who that may be and how to bring them inward. This is a great exercise to visually identify changes that may need to happen. What changes are those?

If you need to build other's trust in you what steps will you take to do so? When will you make a point of doing that this month? What specific things do you need to do or say to increase their trust? How will you know that you have built their trust in you?

If you need to build trust in others what steps will you take to do so? When will you make a point of doing that this month? What specific things do you need to do or say to increase their trust? How will you know that you have built your trust in them?

Deborah R. Monroe

Create your action plan to delegate a project to someone on your team. Remember to follow up with them. Put the time on your calendar, otherwise you may not get to it with your busy schedule.

Project name: Person assigned:			
Item	Resource	Time	Followed up
Asset inventory	Dbase	2 days 2/28/2011	Yes, everything done
Action 1			
Action 2			
Action 3			
Action 4			
Action 5			
Action 6			

Maintenance

> *"Use pain as a stepping stone, not a campground"*
> *— Alan Cohen*

I hope this month was a great learning experience for you. Let's review what you discovered.

What key themes were uncovered concerning control? Where am I at risk of controlling situations more frequently than others?

With that knowledge, what did I begin to change in my approach in those situations?

What do I need to be cognizant of moving forward? Were there particular people, places or situations that triggered me more than others?

Regarding my trust circle, who needed to be moved from one circle to another? What did I do to begin to change that?

Did I begin to build the trust of others? What were the results that I saw?

Did I begin to build the trust that others have in me? How did I do that and how have I seen the change in them?

Concerning my action plan, was I able to delegate a project successfully to someone else? How did it make me feel? What measure of time have I added to my ability to do my strategic planning and other tasks?

What changes have I seen in my team since I began to delegate simple projects?

BLADE #9

Reduce Stress and Get Creative

"Over the years your bodies become walking autobiographies, telling friends and strangers alike of the minor and major stresses of your lives." — Marilyn Ferguson

I like to study stress, mainly because my life has been one big stress production! If it is not one thing, it is another. I settle in, thinking I have everything under control and then, boom, I remember that the car engine light came on yesterday. Now I have to figure out, how I am going to get my car down to the auto shop, take time away from work and throw away five potential work hours by driving down and back to the dealership two times, stand in line, wait for the car to be finished.

I think, "do they have wireless access so I can work? How much is this going to cost me? Do they have a loaner or a rental car that I can use so I can get back to the office? Are they going to fix the problem this time or is it going to reoccur within the next month?" Argh....

In mid thought about the car, someone calls and needs me across the country to teach a class and they need me to leave that afternoon. The doorbell rings in the middle of a coaching call, there is a delivery of a Christmas present and I asked them not to deliver during this time frame because I was on a call. I am hungry. I look through the refrigerator for something, and realize that there is nothing to eat and no sense in buying anything because I will be leaving to the airport in 45 minutes. I race to pack the suitcase, water the plants, make sure the animals have someone to check on them, the bed is made, the house is somewhat clean, the paperwork I need on my journey is packed with the computer and noise-reduction headphones. I bounce upstairs and downstairs with 30 minutes left on the clock. Oops, I need to make reservations for the flight. Same day flights require a phone call the airlines. With urgency and time ticking away I hear the lovely hold music and curse the fact that I have to wait in the call queue for someone to pick up. I walk around the house, getting dressed; putting on my makeup all while the background music is playing on my headset. 15 minutes left before I need to leave for the airport. I do a final check of the house, throw my luggage in the back of the car, tie up the garbage and throw that in the back of the car with the luggage.

The airline agent responds to the urgency in my voice with great understanding leading me to get out my credit card, which is now in the car. I run out to the garage pick up my purse and everything falls out on the floor of the car. I use a little expletive language and then have to apologize to the agent for my rudeness. Ticket's purchased. Triple check of the house. I have everything and I drive off into the sunset for a flight that will get me nowhere because of existing weather! I live for times like these! The adventure, the spontaneity and the stress…

There is so much research on stress and so many great books have been written on the subject I wonder if we need to approach this subject. I will say absolutely, yes! We hear all about stress, yet when it comes to practicing the science of reducing it we largely ignore it or do not understand how to appropriate it for ourselves. Stress reduction is like trying to catch a frightened chicken that is running around the yard. Just when you think you have a good chance of grasping it, it flies away or changes direction and ultimately, you end up with your face in the mud, covered in chicken poop! No fun at all!

So here are some facts about the cost of stress in the workplace:

> Stress cost in the USA, 1986: $75 billion reported in 2005 at $300 billion
>
> Stress cost in Britain, 2005: $200 billion
>
> (Absence from work, health charges, increased insurance and diminished productivity)

In the year 2000:

- $19.4 billion lost by us industry every year due to premature employee death.

- The U.S. due to stress-related absenteeism loses $150 million per year.

- Between 1980-1990, the number of stress disability claims made by California state workers increased by more than 800%.

- $700 million are spent every year to recruit replacements for executives with heart disease.

- Chronic pain, hypertension and headaches (three stress-related disorders) make up 54% of all job absenteeism.

- 40% of employee turnover is due to job stress.

- Worker's compensation awards for job stress are usually four times the awards for regular injury claim.

And this was in the year 2000!

Enough said, stress costs money and of course, costs us so much more within our organizations in the lack of creativity and innovation.

So what is stress? I like this definition:

> *Stress is the psychological and psychosocial reaction that takes place when you perceive an imbalance in the level of demand placed on you and your capacity to meet that demand.*

Or

Demand > Capacity = Stress

My simple definition is that stress is a result of *our inability to deal effectively with change.*

There is of course good stress and unhealthy stress.

Good stress is called **Eustress**. Eustress was coined by Hans Selye in 1974. This is the stress that helps us be productive. It is the stress that gets us out of bed in the morning to brush our teeth and put on clean clothes. My trip to the airport example was a combination of Eustress and unhealthy stress.

The thrill of being able to accommodate my customer on such short notice motivated me right out of the house. I paid for the surge of adrenaline and cortisol (stress chemicals shot through my body and brain during the race) by my inability to sleep during that night. I knew it was coming and nothing, not even a Tylenol pm, could have stopped it!

In my courses I use a custom framework based upon the foundation of the ***General Adaptation Syndrome*** to describe what happens to the body of long periods of stress.

You will note that I have six different areas identified in the cycle. Each one builds on the other unless we take the opportunity to CRASH. When we crash as defined in section one of this workbook, we can ultimately avoid two of the most destructive areas in the cycle, distress and hyper-arousal. Have a look on the next page to discern which part of the cycle you are currently living with and in!

The General Adaptation Cycle of Stress

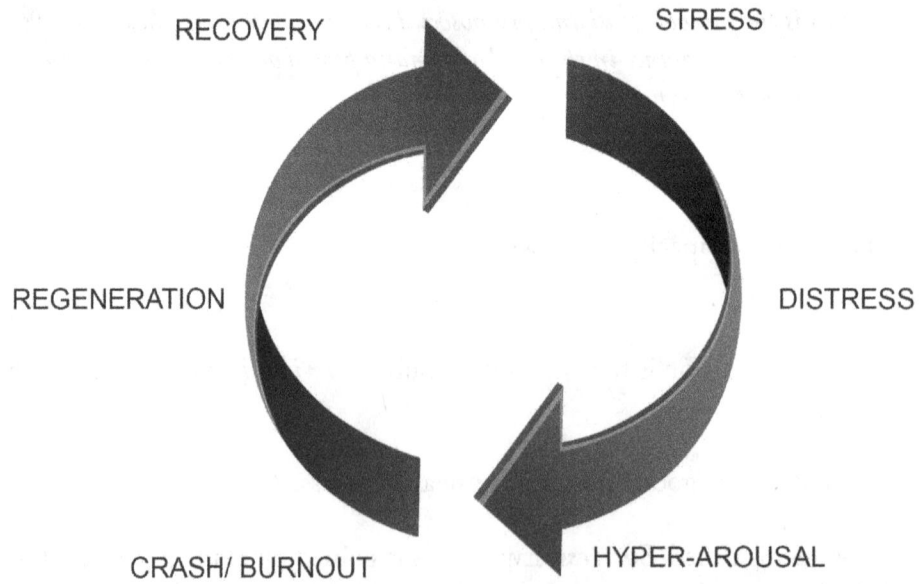

Fortunately, humans have been designed to adapt to stressful symptoms. Many times of crisis and the more serious symptoms of stress can be avoided if we allow ourselves to follow our own biological design. Our bodies have certain amounts of adaptation energy. A biological cache for the times of stress we will encounter; continued stress and unresolved issues use up this reserve. It takes a toll on our physical and emotional self.

Stress symptoms: increased moodiness, increased illness, sleep patterns five to seven hours per night, increase or decrease in appetite, increase in substance abuse, lack of focus, and increase in accidents.

Distress symptoms: stress symptoms on steroids and sleep patterns of three to five hours per night, depression can manifest psychic pain (emotional pain that turns into physical pain), obsessive thoughts or racing mind.

Hyper-arousal: sleep patterns of less than 3 hours, manic behavior (inability to shut down), and greatly obsessive thought patterns.

Crash: a voluntary state that should be practiced in any onset of stress symptoms. This involves giving one's self permission to do what they enjoy or doing nothing at all. It removes all the "I need to's, I have to's, I should do's" from the equation. One should practice crashing at least once a week or once a month.

Burnout: emotionally numb, lethargic, no energy, no creativity, isolation.

Regeneration: relaxing, refocusing, re-energizing. Chemicals such as cortisol coming back into balance.

Recovery: contentment, energy, creativity, hope and freshness.

While you may see stress as a problem, it's also an important tool if you pay attention to the signs! *The emotions of stress are information.*

Stress is like a warning light on your car – it tells you something is at risk. Often it is a warning sign that we have stopped paying attention to who we really are. Once you've identified your stress areas and understood where you are in the stress cycle, the next step is coming back into balance.

So how do we get ourselves back into balance? I have a list that works for me personally. Know that I do take a crash day at least once a week. I give myself permission to do this by speaking out loud, Deborah" I give you permission to take a crash day" so that guilt has no place in my mind. Sometimes during that crash day I will get a glass of wine, a small canvas, some inexpensive brushes and paint, sit at the dinning room table, turn on some Brahms or Mozart and go to town with my artwork. I know that I am not a painter. One of the voices that yells at me when I sit down for this relaxation is my 11th grade art teacher, who in front of the whole class exclaimed loudly that" Deborah, you draw like a six year old". Whether that is true or not, I sit down with no judgment on myself and just paint. Whatever the result does not matter, although one day I hope to have an exhibit at the DIA museum of contemporary and modern art in New York next to the works of Andy Warhol! One can dream, of course!

One of the most important and devastating effects of stress is that it limits our capacity to be creative and innovative. This "right" part of the brain suffers immensely in our "left brain" culture. One of the first things to go in stress is the flow of creativity. For our minds to work at the premium in troubleshooting, problem solving and critical thinking, it is imperative that we make every effort to exercise this creativity. One of the best resources I can suggest for boosting this massively important part of your life is to read **Daniel Pink's** book, *A Whole New Mind, Why Right-Brainers Will Rule The Future*. Then take just one chapter from his book and concentrate on implementing that one thing over the next month.

Here is a small list of balancing techniques and actions that you can incorporate to reduce your stress levels!

- Breathe deeply

- Drink more water

- Eat balanced foods, more small meals

- Hobbies that get you moving

- Laugh

- Write in journal

- Give time to friends & pets

- Go to nature & sunlight

- Feel thankfulness and gratitude

- Take lunch (we already talked about this)

- Take a vacation! You can do this if your inbox is empty and you delegate the task of monitoring that inbox to someone you trust!

I don't believe that we need to get into the science of how stress physically happens and how the brain reacts; the chemicals that run around our destroying brain neurons. What is more important to us here is that now we know where we are in the cycle and we have some tools to begin to manage that stress.

Clean My Tools

"Everything flows and nothing abides; everything gives way and nothing stays fixed... Cool things become warm, the warm grows cool; the moist dries, the parched becomes moist... It is in changing that things find repose." ~
Heraclitus

First things first, this month. Please get your hands on a copy of **Daniel Pink's** book, *A Whole New Mind, Why Right-Brainers Will Rule The Future*.

When you receive it, begin to read it. It will become plain to you as far as which chapter you want to spend time investigating. Dan has given great resources in the back of each section of his book to help you appropriate the learning and make the creative experience valuable.

On the following pages there is a stress assessment. Take the time to complete the assessment and the questions at the end of the assessment.

Schedule time in your calendar to begin one of the changes you want to make. Remember that small incremental consistent changes are the ones that last. This is not a "new year's resolution". We want this change to stick!

Stress Assessment

This questionnaire will help you to pinpoint the areas of your life where stress is occurring. Choose yes or no to the following questions.

© 2010 Ignite Achievements Int'l 2001 written by Sally Wright and used with permission. Updated 2006-12 Deborah R. Monroe

Assessing stress		
	Yes	No
Your environment		
Are you running out of room to put things?		
Is your home too small and cramped?		
Do you feel that you don't have enough privacy?		
Do you find it difficult to relax at home in the evenings?		
Are your neighbors too noisy?		
Do you feel depressed in the dark winter months?		
Do you wake up in the morning with a stiff back?		
Do you feel uncomfortable after sitting for a long period?		
Do you like where you live or would you prefer to move?		
Do you have a long commute?		
Yourself		
Do you feel trapped in a set of circumstances you cannot change?		
Do you feel like you have many faults and a few good points?		
Do you feel like you are fooling everyone with what you know and who you are?		
Do you often suppress your own views because you think others will be offended?		
Do you often give up something you want to do because of what others want?		

Do you spend a lot of time worrying about the future?		
Do you loose your temper easily?		
Do you find it difficult to relax?		
Do you pre judge situations and then find out that you were mistaken?		
Do you find it hard to say you are sorry?		
Your relationships		
Do you find that you never have any time for yourself?		
Do you argue a lot about money?		
Do you feel that you don't have enough privacy at home?		
Are you finding it difficult to settle down into a permanent relationship?		
Is your family resentful that you don't spend enough time at home?		
Is it hard for you to forgive?		
Do you bring past relationship issues into your current one?		
Do you tell the truth when you are upset or hide it to avoid conflict?		
Do you feel that others are controlling and you don't have a choice?		
Do you find it a problem when children answer back or are rude to you?		
Your job		
Do you feel put-upon or feel you are working too hard?		
Do you regularly work during lunchtimes or evenings?		
Do you rarely take vacations?		
Do you get a depressed feeling when you wake up and think you have to go to work?		
Do you feel bored with your job?		
Do you find it difficult to organize your work?		
Do you find it difficult to delegate work to someone else when you get busy?		
Do you find that constant interruptions ruin your concentration?		

Do you feel your talents or abilities are not fully recognized?		
Do you feel listened to by your manager?		
Time management		
Do you usually try to do things as quickly as possible?		
Do you run out of time when working on important projects?		
Do you deliberately try to do several things at once?		
Have you noticed that you are forgetting things of late?		
Do you get impatient easily?		
Do you always travel to work during rush hour?		
Do you only rarely give yourself a break to play, relax, or daydream?		
Are you so busy with operations that you don't spend enough time thinking strategically?		
Do you rarely use a diary or a journal to write your thoughts in?		
Are you aware that time is passing too quickly?		
Diet and exercise		
Do you regularly take less that half an hour for main meals?		
Do you often eat while doing other things like cooking or working?		
Do you eat high calorie foods that produce an instant energy high?		
Do you drink more than 3 cups of coffee or tea a day?		
Do you drink more than 2 glasses of wine or bottles of beer a day?		
Do you put on weight easily or quickly?		
Do you smoke?		
Do you never set aside some time every day for yourself?		
Do your daily activities rarely include some degree of physical exertion?		
Do you drink less than 8 glasses of water every day?		
Total the number of "yes" answers		

Identify the percentage of stress in your life

50-60 yes's	100% of your life is stressed
35-49 yes's	80% of your life is stressed
24-34 yes's	50% of your life is stressed
14-23 yes's	25% of your life is stressed
Under 14	your life is a breeze!

Identify the area that has the most stress. Tally the yes's for each section. Make a note of which area is the most difficult for you to manage at this time.

Your environment   _____

Yourself   _____

Your relationships   _____

Your job   _____

Your time management'   _____

Your diet and exercise   _____

Notes:

Action Plan

List one small item that you can change in each area listed:

Health

Environment

Work

Deborah R. Monroe

Family

Financial

Don't forget to define times when you will implement the changes and define how you know you will have been successful!

Remember things that made you happy; ideas, passions, desires that you placed in the back of your mind or put on hold. Then identify ways to bring them back to life here and now.

Idea 1 _____

How will I revive this? How will this idea look today? What do I need to do to implement it? What resources will I need? Who do I need to contact?

Idea 2 _____

How will I revive this? How will this idea look today? What do I need to do to implement it? What resources will I need? Who do I need to contact?

Deborah R. Monroe
_____

Idea 3 _____

How will I revive this? How will this idea look today? What do I need to do to implement it? What resources will I need? Who do I need to contact?

_____

_____

_____

Maintenance

"Creativity is piercing the mundane to find the marvelous."
— Bill Moyers

The things we fear most in organizations — fluctuations, disturbances, imbalances — are the primary sources of creativity." — Margaret J. Wheatley

Which chapter in **Daniel Pink's** book did you choose to reflect upon and put action to?

Have you noticed a difference in your ability to concentrate and become creative because of participating in that activity?

After taking the stress assessment, what actions did you take to relieve the stress in one particular area? What area was that in?

How have you applied stress reduction in your life the last month?

Which ideas, passions, and desires from your past did you identify and bring back to life? What did it feel like to identify them and begin to implement them?

What is the one proudest accomplishment that you accomplished this month?

BLADE #10

Kindness Is The fertilizer That Makes Things Grow!

"Life's most urgent question is: "What are you doing for others?"
— Martin Luther King, Jr.

The first task of a leader is to define reality. The last is to say thank you. — Max Dupree

The opportunity to be kind is around every corner, even if it does not manifest itself fully in these days and times. I want to be one who extends kindness as many times a day as possible, even if only with a smile. There is brilliance in kindness that shows in a soul. It shines through one's eyes and on the countenance of the face. I too, like Blanche Dubois in the movie, *A Street Car Named Desire*, "Depend upon the kindness of strangers"!

Kindness at its heart is the act of helpfulness towards someone in need with no strings attached or done for the advantage of the helper, although there are benefits that do arise when the act of kindness is received. The point is that none should be expected.

Kindness is also attached to the emotion of Empathy, which in a past section in this workbook has been defined and shown as something that has been greatly lacking in our working and personal environments. There is no way to satisfy our craving to receive kindness except to be the first to give it and then watch the changes happen around us.

Kindness does not mend all offenses. In fact, it has the slight possibility of creating them, but that is another story. I can tell you that I can recount almost every time that someone reached out to me when I was in need. They are illuminated and posed in my memory like works of art in a museum.

Deborah R. Monroe

All of us have heard the saying, "Go the extra mile", yet few of us know where that phrase comes from or what was really meant by it. Here is a little history lesson.

As I understand it and history tells us, over 2000 years ago, the Romans ruled the world. What were the Romans famous for, besides killing people? They were famous for their engineering and their road building capabilities. "All roads lead to Rome" is a wonderful reminding quote. Their roads were perfectly engineered, not off in the slightest degree and of course, they did not have a GPS to attach to the oxen's horns! I have a GPS and still get lost! The Romans were clever; they put Roman mile markers at every Roman mile, which is more equivalent to a kilometer than a North American mile. Some of the roads they built 2000 years ago are still visible and some still traveled today in Europe and the Middle East. That is a heritage in my mind!

The story begins in Palestine all those years ago. The Jews were considered to be slaves under Roman rule. The rule of law at the time stated that if you were a Jewish slave working your sheep, land or simply passing by and you saw a Roman Soldier standing by one of these Roman mile markers, it was your obligation to leave your sheep, land or family. You were to walk up to the Soldier, pick up their belongings, which could have weighed up to one hundred pounds (or 43 kilos) and then escort the Roman to the next mile marker. At that point, you were obligated to go no farther; you could drop their luggage and go back to your sheep! Such was life.

In the story told by Jesus, He said, "If someone compels you to go one mile, go two". What gets left behind in translation here is that, yes, you have to go the obligatory mile, yet, when you decide to go the farther distance, something in the relationship changes.

In our chronicle of the "extra mile", during the first mile, the slave remains a slave and the Roman soldier remains conqueror. When the slave passes the first mile marker and unexpectedly continues the journey, the voyage of obligation is finished and the journey of the heart begins.

When that occurs the relationship between the two people in the story changes. There is no longer a slave and a conqueror walking down a dusty road. There are now two men walking side by side down that road. This opens the opportunity for discussion that would unlikely happen during the first mile. The slave can then talk and the conqueror must listen.

The slave will talk about his life, his family, his values, and who his people are and what they believe. The Roman is obligated to listen. The dynamic that happens in this part of the journey is that empathy is built with the slave population; understanding is grown and the slave is seen as a human being with the same human struggles as the Roman soldier standing next to him. It is always suggested to keep your friends close and your enemies closer and doing this creates the space for that to happen. In fact, it may turn an enemy closer and into a friend.

In our going about day-to-day, relationships do become strained as agendas and egos seem to take on the attribute of a solar flare. A simple act of kindness can douse that flame of heat.

Dennis was one of my direct reports   He was one of those people that I knew I should not have hired. His behavior was stubborn, rebellious and his attitude was negative and dangerous. Every task that was assigned to him was received with complaint and gruff acknowledgment. It wore me down until I threw my hands up in frustration and disgust. Yes, those are strong words, yet they capture the moment with truth and clarity. Instead of fighting fire with fire, I thought to send Dennis a thank you in an e-card for all the work he had accomplished. I wanted to show him that I truly appreciated what he had done in the past, although I always made a point of saying that to him on a daily basis verbally. There was a knock on my office door. Dennis stepped in with a completely different repose that I was used to seeing. He stumbled with his words asking if I had sent that e-card to him. His face softened, his eyes lightened and a swift one sided smile flashed passed my desk. That card made such a difference to him and to me. Cooperation began to settle itself into the office and for a time we had a bond that encouraged both of us to get along with one another and work towards the same goals without crashing into one another like stick and piñata (me being the piñata)!

Another great story comes from my father. He spent years in the corporate world working his way from a lowly programmer at IBM to a V.P. and then at his own company. One of the things that I can tell you is that he was gone from home a great deal in my youth. Most weeks were spent in quality time with just my mom. Dad came home for the weekends. Not only was he working hard and late, but also his whole team did the same.

I remember listening to him tell a story about his employees working extensively and traveling all week long. In that case dad would send a dozen roses to their wives with a note of appreciation and thanks. Understanding that it was not only the gentleman that worked hard, but so did she, as the wife did as well, holding down the fort all week long while her husband was gone. Dad did the same for the female employees working with him. He sent their husbands a bottle of Scotch or a reservation for two to a fine local restaurant, as to say, "We could not do this without you and I want you to know that I know that"! In doing this Pop created an environment for his staff that set expectations of value, not only to the employees themselves, but also to the families involved. I was so taken back by this; I wondered why his managers never did that for my mother! It would have certainly made her week handling her crazy children much more bearable!

We cannot forget that one of the prevalent places to acknowledge kindness is upon your own person. I don't mean to go out and buy a new car or a week in the Bahamas, though that would be very nice! I do mean that kindness to oneself begins with what is going on in your head. By this time you should be aware of all the merciless thoughts that you have towards yourself. We can be have greater meanness and be more difficult on our own person than with other people. If you are still struggling with that, it is time to really take a long look at why, what it sounds like and finally, put it to death. It is not serving you well at all and is so very destructive.

One of the discoveries I made several years ago was the work of Dr. Masaru Emoto. His work is displayed in one of his many books entitled, **Messages from Water**. Dr. Emoto began to study water and its reaction to words that were either thought or spoken over the water. As a scientist, Dr. Emoto always did a baseline test. He would take a water molecule and freeze it; then study the water molecule under a microscope. His discovery took place when he taped a word like "thanksgiving" or "love" inward facing on a glass of water, then froze that water to study the crystalline shape of the water molecule. The molecule changed into an amazing and beautiful configuration. The same experiment was conducted when he used words that we consider to be negative like "war or "anger". The water molecules would become deformed and almost sludgy in appearance. Truly, that is what happened!

Suffice to say that lean muscle tissue contains about 99% water by weight. Blood contains almost 70% water, body fat contains 10% water and bone has 22% water. Skin also contains much water. The human body is about 60% water in adult males and 55% in adult females and 75% in children. (source Wikipedia).

In translation, if our bodies contain so much water and the science seems to prove that it reacts to our words, the question arises, are we walking around with sludge or active crystalline molecular structure that creates health and sense? As far as I can see, it makes great wisdom to speak nicely to ourselves, not only for physical, but also for our mental health.

Some kindness can be considered harsh as well. We do need to understand that not all forms of kindness are healthy. Kindness brought to a fault can be considered enablement. As with anything, it is important to strike a balance. No doubt you have heard the phrase, "be kind and put them out of their misery"! One of the greatest acts of kindness that anyone ever performed for me was personally devastating in its emotion. It didn't seem kind at the time as the receiver. It was also very difficult for them; I know they struggled with the decision to the point of pain. Yet, after all was said and done and years passed; the pain was replaced by wisdom. I realized that I would never be where I am today, had I not allowed that difficult act of kindness to grow my character. I did call the person and thank them for being so brave and sticking to their decision. Kindness in that fashion may come disguised in a black suite with a death mask! I encourage you to look back at situations and events in your life that at that time seemed to rip your heart apart and come to an understanding that it was for the best and growth comes from it.

Kindness comes in many forms. It can be in the form of a smile and a nod; the form of an unexpected gift; someone helping you on the side of the road when your car breaks down; someone releasing you from a debt that would take you years to pay. Kindness can be in the form of volunteering your time or energy; a simple phone call to catch up; or a thank you card. It can also take the form of harsh words or decisions that are difficult to swallow. Whatever form it takes, we do it with no expectations and no strings attached. We do it because it is the right thing to do, the human thing to do and it will create a place for relationship and growth in others and ourselves.

Deborah R. Monroe

Clean My Tools

> *"Constant kindness can accomplish much. As the sun makes ice melt, kindness causes misunderstanding, mistrust, and hostility to evaporate."* — Albert Schweitzer

Let's discover this:

What act of kindness was done to me in the last three years that really is memorable? How did it make me feel? What was the lasting impact of this act on you me

How have I reciprocated that act of kindness to another? How did it make me feel? What was the lasting impact of that act on the other person?

This month list one act of kindness that I will perform for each group of people. Include what it is and when I will do it:

Your Parents?

Your Partner?

Your Children?

Your Co-Workers?

Your Manager?

Your Direct Reports?

Yourself?

Someone specifically I am having a challenge with, by name?

What words have I noticed that I am using to describe myself that are not encouraging and uplifting?

_____

_____

_____

How will I "catch" those negative words and what positive phrase will I replace them with?

_____

_____

_____

How will I know you have been successful in clearing my mind of those negative voices that speak to me harshly? Think about this one; don't give a "pat" answer.

_____

_____

_____

Maintenance

"You can accomplish by kindness what you cannot by force."
— *Publius Cornelius Tacitus*

Over the last month, what was your proudest moment in giving kindness?

Did you see a change in any of the relationships where an act of kindness was delivered? What were they?

How do you want to continue this attitude of kindness and gratitude?

Deborah R. Monroe

What have you done for yourself and what have been the greatest change in you?

BLADE #11

Review of the Year

It has been an amazing journey. The honor is mine to share these straightforward and yet challenging concepts. I trust that you were able to complete every month and watch yourself and those around you grow in ways that you had only hoped. Do drop me an email to share one of your amazing stories. We will post it on the website anonymously if you like!

As a wrap up, take an hour or so to do a simple review of what impacted you the most each month. What was your big take away in each section? What changes did you see within yourself and those around you? What do you need to do to keep each month's learning alive and active in your life? Which area do you want to continue working on in depth?

Blade #1: Honor Myself

What was your big take away in this section?

Deborah R. Monroe

What changes did you see within yourself and those around you?

_____
_____
_____
_____

What do you need to do to keep this section's learning alive and active in your life?

_____
_____
_____
_____

Which area do you want to continue working on in depth?

_____
_____
_____
_____

Blade #2: Manage My Distractions

What was your big take away in this section?

What changes did you see within yourself and those around you?

What do you need to do to keep this section's learning alive and active in your life?

Which area do you want to continue working on in depth?

Blade #3: Get Myself a Coach

What was your big take away in this section?

What changes did you see within yourself and those around you?

What do you need to do to keep this section's learning alive and active in your life?

_____
_____
_____
_____

Which area do you want to continue working on in depth?

_____
_____
_____
_____

Blade #4: The Art of Listening

What was your big take away in this section?

_____
_____
_____
_____

Deborah R. Monroe

What changes did you see within yourself and those around you?

What do you need to do to keep this section's learning alive and active in your life?

Which area do you want to continue working on in depth?

Blade #5: What is "Coming Out" of My Mouth

What was your big take away in this section?

What changes did you see within yourself and those around you?

What do you need to do to keep this section's learning alive and active in your life?

Which area do you want to continue working on in depth?

Blade #6: Build My Relationships

What was your big take away in this section?

What changes did you see within yourself and those around you?

What do you need to do to keep this section's learning alive and active in your life?

Which area do you want to continue working on in depth?

Blade #7: Manage My Thought Life

What was your big take away in this section?

What changes did you see within yourself and those around you?

What do you need to do to keep this section's learning alive and active in your life?

Which area do you want to continue working on in depth?

Blade #8: Let Go and Delegate

What was your big take away in this section?

What changes did you see within yourself and those around you?

What do you need to do to keep this section's learning alive and active in your life?

Which area do you want to continue working on in depth?

Blade #9: Reduce Stress and Get Creative

What was your big take away in this section?

What changes did you see within yourself and those around you?

What do you need to do to keep this section's learning alive and active in your life?

Which area do you want to continue working on in depth?

Blade #10: Kindness Is The Fertilizer That Makes Everything Grow!

What was your big take away in this section?

What changes did you see within yourself and those around you?

What do you need to do to keep this section's learning alive and active in your life?

Which area do you want to continue working on in depth?

Appendix A:

Accountability Coach Guidelines

Here are some guidelines if budget has limited you and you need to seek out an Accountability Partner instead of hiring a coach. You may want to copy this page, encouraging the accountability partner to use these strategies.

It is in the best interest of your coach/accountability partner to review and do this workbook with you so that they understand the concepts being referenced.

Your coach/accountability partner will be a master question asker. You are seeking someone to ask you questions, not tell you what they think is the right or wrong approach.

- They should have a natural inquisitive nature

- They should be trustworthy, of great character and integrity

- All coaches/accountability partners should consider the conversation sacrosanct (confidential and sacred).

- They should not offer any advice or opinion unless you specifically ask them to give you advice or opinion

- Criticism or "feedback" is not acceptable in coaching unless you ask for it to be given to you. Unless the person has responsibility in your life, and you have given permission, they do not have the authority to do so.

- Enthusiasm should mark successes you have made. Take time to celebrate with your coach/partner

- Assurance should mark struggles you are working through. Encouragement goes farther to breed success than any other approach.

- If either of you are uncomfortable at any point, stay honest; tell your truth. Not every coach or accountability partner is a good match. The relationship could work for a time and then not be effective after a while. It is okay to part ways if that happens. Glean from the experience and move ahead.

- Don't take everything too seriously. Tell stories with one another and share both your successes and failures. This is one of the greatest ways to learn.

- Enjoy the process and watch as everyone who goes through this with you grows too!

Interviewing Potential Coaches/Accountability Partners:

1. Ask how long they have been a coach? Are they certified by any organization?

2. Ask what motivated them in becoming a coach? Why do they enjoy coaching?

3. Ask if there are any potential biases they may have based on culture or experience.

4. What areas of coaching have they practiced at i.e., corporate setting, educational, or a more relaxed environment such as a sport team or spiritual environment such as a youth group etc.

5. Are they flexible in the location of coaching or performing the sessions over the phone.

6. Will they provide some examples of their coaching strategies or techniques?

7. Of course their hourly rate or contractual rate and specifically what this entails. (scheduled meetings, phone calls, strategic planning, review of outline plan etc.)

Appendix B:

List Of Emotions And Feelings

Source: The Center Of Nonviolent Communication
(C) 2005 By Center For Nonviolent Communication
Website: www.cnvc.org email: *cnvc@cnvc.org*
Phone: +1.505.244.4041

Affectionate
compassionate
friendly
loving
open-hearted
sympathetic
tender
warm

confident
empowered
open
proud
safe
secure

engaged
absorbed
alert
curious
engrossed
enchanted
entranced
fascinated
interested
intrigued
involved
spellbound
stimulated

inspired
amazed
awed
wonder

Excited
amazed
animated
ardent
aroused
astonished
dazzled
eager
energetic
enthusiastic
giddy
invigorated
lively
passionate
surprised
vibrant

exhilarated
blissful
ecstatic
elated
enthralled
exuberant
radiant
rapturous
thrilled

grateful
appreciative
moved
thankful
touched

hopeful
expectant
encouraged
optimistic

Joyful
amused
delighted
glad
happy
jubilant
pleased
tickled

peaceful
calm
clear-headed
comfortable
centered
content
equanimous
fulfilled
mellow
quiet
relaxed
relieved
satisfied
serene
still
tranquil
trusting

refreshed
enlivened
rejuvenated
renewed
rested
restored
revived

Feelings when your needs are not satisfied

Afraid
apprehensive
dread
foreboding
frightened
mistrustful
panicked
petrified
scared
suspicious
terrified
wary
worried

annoyed
aggravated
dismayed
disgruntled
displeased
exasperated
frustrated
impatient
irritated
irked
angry
enraged
furious
incensed
indignant
irate
livid
outraged
resentful

aversion
animosity
appalled
contempt
disgusted
dislike
hate
horrified
hostile
repulsed

confused
ambivalent
baffled
bewildered
dazed
hesitant
lost
mystified
perplexed
puzzled
torn

Disconnected
alienated
aloof
apathetic
bored
cold
detached
distant
distracted
indifferent
numb
removed
uninterested
withdrawn

disquiet
agitated
alarmed
discombobulated
disconcerted
disturbed
perturbed
rattled
restless
shocked
startled
surprised
troubled
turbulent
turmoil
uncomfortable
uneasy
unnerved
unsettled
upset

embarrassed
ashamed
chagrined
flustered
guilty
mortified
self-conscious

fatigue
beat
burnt-out
depleted
exhausted
lethargic
listless
sleepy
tired
weary
worn out

Pain
agony
anguished
bereaved
devastated
grief
heartbroken
hurt
lonely
miserable
regretful
remorseful

sad
depressed
dejected
despair
despondent
disappointed
discouraged
disheartened
forlorn
gloomy
heavy-hearted
hopeless
melancholy
unhappy
wretched

tense
anxious
cranky
distressed
distraught
edgy
fidgety
frazzled
irritable
jittery
nervous
overwhelmed
restless
stressed-out

vulnerable
fragile
guarded
helpless
insecure
leery
reserved
sensitive
shaky

yearning
envious
jealous
longing
nostalgic
pining
wistful

Appendix C:

List Of Human Needs

Source: the center of nonviolent communication

(c) 2005 by center for nonviolent communication

Website: www.cnvc.org email: cnvc@cnvc.org

Phone: +1.505.244.4041

The following list of needs is neither exhaustive nor definitive. It is meant as a starting place to support anyone who wishes to engage in a process of deepening self-discovery and to facilitate greater understanding and connection between people.

Connection
acceptance
affection
appreciation
belonging
cooperation
communication
closeness
community
companionship
compassion
consideration
consistency
empathy
inclusion
intimacy
love
mutuality
nurturing
respect/self-respect
safety
security
stability
support
to know and be known
to see and be seen
to understand and be understood
trust
warmth

Physical well-being
air
food
movement/exercise
rest/sleep
sexual-expression
safety
shelter
touch
water

honesty
authenticity
integrity
presence

play
joy
humor

peace
beauty
communion
ease
equality
harmony
inspiration
order

Meaning
awareness
celebration–of–life
challenge
clarity
competence
consciousness
contribution
creativity
discovery
efficacy
effectiveness
growth
hope
learning
mourning
participation
purpose
self-expression
stimulation
understanding

autonomy
choice
freedom
independence
space
spontaneity

Appendix D:

Things To Consider List!

1. We all need coaches!
2. Even if it makes your toes curl under, be honest with yourself.
3. Even if it makes your hair curl, be honest with others.
4. You don't have to control everything.
5. We need to work on trusting others and their abilities.
6. You can only be strategic thinker when you don't have to micro-manage the operations.
7. Email your coach with your latest challenge.
8. When you get all these things sorted out it is highly likely that you will be promoted….or want a new job!
9. The reason that they won't listen to you is….they have no reason to… give them a reason…if you don't know what that is, call your coach.
10. Please do your assignments.
11. God gave us two ears and one mouth. Some say because we should be listening twice as much as we should be talking or others say it is twice as hard to listen as it is to talk.
12. It's not all about you all the time.
13. Socialize for 2 minutes before you get down to business.
14. Look up from your work when someone comes into your office and asks you a question.
15. Be present, if you don't know how call your coach.
16. Be self aware of your facial expressions and the way you react to situations and people.
17. Do you have favorites?
18. Sarcasm is still the lowest form of wit and will eventually offend and alienate someone who is or will be important to you.
19. Be aware of your physical self when you get upset, make a note of what is going on in your body. Next time it happens breathe and focus.
20. If an email triggers you, don't respond right away. Let it sit until you can think clearly about it without feeling tension, then respond.
21. Assess when you are at greatest risk for an emotional hijack and plan in advance so you know you are not blindsided.
22. Turn the adrenaline rush into an endorphin rush.
23. Learn what motivates your peers and employees.

24. Understand your employee's basic personality styles.
25. Find out how your manager likes to communicate and communicate with them in that way.
26. Always meet with you manager at least once every two weeks.
27. Meet with your team leads or project managers once a week.
28. Go out of your way to be caring.
29. Take your team out for dinner once a quarter.
30. Develop career paths if you are able.
31. Teach your team to give you solutions not problems.
32. The warm and fuzzy stuff matters.
33. You have the power to build up or destroy.
34. Learn how to coach your problem children, call your coach if you need help.
35. Mercy triumphs over judgment.
36. Involve your team in decisions to gain respect and buy in.
37. Always be on time to meetings.
38. Building up your team increases your chance of a promotion.
39. If you are not happy, do something else.
40. Don't gossip or create strife, it is really ugly and immature.
41. You create the "field" of energy you work in and others can feel it.
42. Your emotions spread, what are you spreading?
43. You are really only one person; act like it, the congruence of your personality depends upon it.
44. Don't be so paranoid.
45. If there is unresolved issues deal with it right away.
46. Fear must be stood up against, even if it is only in your head.
47. Some relationships can be let go of.
48. Don't work for money.
49. If you make, a mistake fess up.
50. Forgive yourself.
51. Forgive others.
52. If you have had enough then say it.
53. Don't be afraid to hurt others feelings.
54. Don't be afraid that you will look stupid, if you do, who cares.
55. If they have it in for you, there is nothing you can do except smile.
56. What goes around comes around, not that you would wish anything bad on someone, it is simple physics!
57. Use your gut instinct.
58. Never loose eye contact.

59. Always give a nice firm handshake. It represents your word.
60. The eyes are the windows of the soul.
61. Many streams are affected with one change. Home vs. Personal life.
62. Don't have a relationship with someone at work…please.
63. Do not drink at company parties or events, you will eventually be sorry you did.
64. Never hire friends or family, unless you own a family business.
65. Just because you have the title of a manager doesn't mean you are.
66. A manager is not a leader.
67. Not everyone needs all the details.
68. People really can't read your mind so tell them what you expect of them.
69. If you are not happy with performance then say something.
70. Start a difficult conversation by stating your intentions.
71. Don't play the blame game, make a decision based upon the outcome you are looking for.
72. If you are not a detail-oriented person realize that others are and give them the time and attention they need to be comfortable.
73. Always use "mirroring" for communication.
74. Understand that we all filter communication thru our experiences.
75. Create action lists.
76. Sometimes it is not people it is processes that are the problem.
77. Perception is reality.
78. Ability doesn't count if no one can see it.
79. Empathy, empathy, empathy.
80. Don't submit to peer pressure.
81. Take your vacation.
82. Take your lunch hour.
83. Make room for life.
84. Do not enable bad behavior in any manager, no matter how much revenue they drive or how much they are responsible for.
85. Your coach has expectations of you.
86. If you don't want the details, tell them!
87. Be honest with grace.
88. Season your speech with salt so it is more palatable for those listening.
89. Turn off your blasted mobile device.
90. Live your life to the fullest. Get out there and taste it!

Contact

For Further information about Ignite Achievements Int'l go to:

www.IgniteAchievements.com

To Reserve Deborah Monroe for Speaking Engagements, Leadership Conferences, Program Facilitation or Emotional Intelligence Coaching email:

ask@IgniteAchievements.com

You can purchase this book for your managers and team by going to:

www.CuttingThroughToSuccess.com

www.ingramcontent.com/pod-product-compliance
Lightning Source LLC
Chambersburg PA
CBHW080336170426
43194CB00014B/2580